LIVENEW

a 31 day life trajectory experiment

by Kurt Libby

THIS BOOK IS DEDICATED TO MY FRIENDS
SHAWN, CASEY, JOSH, & MATT.
OLD IS OVER. JESUS IS LORD. LIVE NEW.

TABLE OF EXPERIMENTS

INTRODUCTION

START HERE

This is a life trajectory experiment. It is written for men and will forego the fluff that makes things sound nice. It cuts to the chase. It deals with reality without any apologies. It is intended for men that have decided to follow Jesus but are frustrated with the lack of real change in their lives. They say that they want God, but this is not evident by the way they live. There isn't a huge difference between their life before meeting Jesus and their life after meeting Jesus. Nothing too drastic has changed. When they look at the end of their lives and hope to be powerful men of God, they wonder how that could ever happen given the current trajectory of their lives. The most common thread among men in this boat is that they do not spend a significant amount of time with Jesus on a daily basis. That is the goal of this book. Significant time with Jesus every day for 31 days. This book cannot change you. God can. This book is intended to help you spend time with Him and work His words into your life. This book is intended to show you that God has called you and enabled you to live new.

WHY

Because deciding to change and actually changing are drastically different. How many times have we decided that we were going to stop, going to start, that things would be different this time and then they aren't. How many times? We can't count that high.

We need help. We were never supposed to fix ourselves. If you think that you can, your view of your self is way too big. But more than that, your view of the Holy Spirit (HS) is way too small. Way. Too. Small.

Get over yourself. You aren't able.

He is able.

Period.

You need this book because no one is standing in front of you, telling you to wake up and proceeding to love you with a generous left hook.

You need this book because you seriously lack discipline.

Change doesn't happen over night. Habits (scientifically) take at least 21 days to develop. Good and bad habits. You can do the things you've always done, but you will get the results you've always gotten.

Jesus looks at your life and sees potential based on His power, not your past. That's why Simon Peter drops his nets, and walks out of his old life to follow Jesus. Later, Peter goes back to fishing, Jesus goes and gets him, calls him out again, recommissions him and sends him out into the world as a representative of the very Son of God.

That's why you need this book. You've heard about Jesus. You've encountered Jesus. But you're holding onto your old life in some way, and the weight is more than just some fishing nets. It pisses you off. It feels like a vomit storm in your gut. You know that Jesus climbed on the cross to set you free, but you have settled for an existence marked more by frustration than freedom.

He has called you out, and you've got to quit your old life. Step out, step up, and step into the life that He is calling you into. No more faking it. This just got real.

WHAT

First things first. Make a commitment in total surrender to God. If you don't start with the fact that Jesus came to be the Lord of your life, then this is just some self-help garbage that will leave you feeling informed and powerless. Jesus has all the authority and all the power and wants to climb your steps and dethrone your ego and run your life. All of it. Sin. Love. Hate. Sex. Finances. Free time. Power. Reactions. Success. Catastrophe. Bravery. Responsibilities. Comforts. Discomforts. Thoughts. Desires. Actions. Everything.

If you want to hold anything back, get a different book. This isn't for you right now. You are your own god. You will probably die serving yourself. You will not save yourself. And that's on you.

But if you're in. All in. Surrendered. Committed. Then let me explain to you how this commitment stuff works.

1. Commit to time. That means putting something that you currently spend time doing daily on your To Don't List. I don't care what it is, but it has to be real. Write it down. Schedule time that you read this book and do what it says instead of that thing. One hour, every day for a whole month. Do not miss a day. If you can't find time in 24 hours to make this a priority, you're not ready. Come back to

this book when you've got courage enough to quit something.

2. Get a Bible. Seriously. If you don't have a Bible that you read all the time, then go out and buy one. Buy a nice one. NIV, ESV, MSG, NLT, whatever. Spend more money on it than you spent on the last thing you bought for yourself. Leather bound. Case. Invest in this. I know you have an app with 30 versions at your fingertips or that Bible that sits on your book shelf, but this needs to cost you something.

3. Get a journal. Again, I'm serious. Moleskin, composition, college ruled, whatever. If you don't write well, I don't care. If you don't journal, I don't care. You do now. Unedited real thoughts and prayers. You are going to write down a lot of real stuff because it helps you slow down and talk to God for longer than 42 seconds (the average length of serious prayers by distracted people). When you write down prayers to God you can literally feel your heart and mind change as you honestly record what is in you and invite Him to transform your heart and mind.

4. Tell someone. You spent $7 on this book (or someone else did for you). If you don't tell anyone that you're going through it and that they can ask you at any point in the next 31 days how it is going, then you may as well have thrown the money in the trash. Have some freaking courage and tell someone that you're investing real time and money

in seeing God powerfully move in your life because you are sick and tired of deciding to follow Jesus instead of actually following Him. Text or call them now.

5. Get on your face when you pray. I'm talking real carpet imprints on your forehead. I'm talking about cutting off the circulation at your knees. I'm talking about uncomfortable absolute reverence for the fact that you are addressing the God of creation, the Lord of all nations. Show some physical respect and expect your heart to follow, not the other way around.

HOW

Everyday. Read it. Sink in it. Pray it. Live it. (RSPL) No make up days. Schedule it as if it was the most important thing in your life. And then make it a priority. If you remember when you're climbing into bed at night, get out of bed, repent for not making it a priority, and RSPL. What do you have to lose? A lot. Your entire old life (which is dead by the way, so let it go–people that cling to death are disgusting) for starters. What do you have to gain? More. More than you could ask or imagine. Because as you surrendered your life to Christ, your sins (with all the guilt and shame) were taken away and you were given His righteousness and the very HS of God. The HS is powerful and active in your life. Act like it. Invest in it.

Learn about who you are now. You are brand freaking new. I've watched my kids discover who they are as they move through their first years in life. It's an adventure. They are always learning, always discovering, always wondering. Even if you've been following Christ for years, you barely know the first thing about what Christ has done in you and who He is making you into. Own that reality and approach the RSPL with the mindset of an infant, hoping to discover who you are because you are brand new. If there are parts in the reading style or journaling or living that are uncomfortable for you, that's ok. Get over it. Do the things that are uncomfortable.

But most of all, be changed. Again, have some freaking courage. Be different. When you feel the HS shifting your mind and transforming your heart, let it happen. And when people say, "Since when were you like that?" Tell them, "Since Tuesday." Or whatever day you were changed.

We live in a Christian culture that believes the lie that generally, Christians don't change. Don't buy it. You've got the HS. The guiding Spirit of God is in you and steering your life. You are marked by change. You are known by love now. You never were before. It's Him in you. Let it happen. Be different.

Jesus didn't die on a cross to get you into heaven after you sucked at life. It was for freedom that Christ set you free. Get ready, because God is getting a grip on your heart, and He is going to wring glory out of your life. He's going to set you free. It's going to hurt. It's going to hurt so good. Over and over and over and over again. He's about to love the hell out of you.

And you will never be the same.

IMAGINE

READ IT

Paul prays for the Christians in Ephesus in Ephesians 3:16-21. Read the prayer right now.

Just to set the stage, you have to understand that Paul's mission in life before meeting Jesus was to destroy Christians. Understand that Paul's life didn't turn out the way he wanted because Jesus stepped in, wrecked him, put him back together, and gave him a new heart and a new mission. So when he prays that they will know this love that surpasses knowledge, this love that has these extravagant dimensions, this love that is too great to understand fully, he is praying this because his mind has been blown. He had been raised very religious and was convinced that God didn't love outsiders. But not only does God love outsiders, He loves insiders that hate outsiders. He loves everyone. His love is indescribably big.

So Paul end's the prayer with verses 20 and 21. Go back and read those again.

SINK IN IT

He throws out the word "imagine." Some translations say "more than all we could ask or imagine."

Question. Where does imagination end? Imagination was created by God. God gave us imagination deep in our souls to assure us of His nature–never ending, infinite, forever and ever (as if forever wasn't enough).

Answer. It doesn't. But we stop. We stop imagining. We convince ourselves that we know every outcome based on logic and experience. Most of the time we don't ask because we have become secretly convinced that God can't do more.

Spend some time sinking in these verses and letting these verses sink in. His glory. His ability. His power. Within us. Allow your mind to be blown. Go back and sink in each phrase in the prayer. Sink in it and imagine what life might look like if God can do more.

PRAY IT

What are the things in your life that you haven't brought to God? List them out and repent. Bring them to God. Ask. He can do more.

But understand this. It begins and ends with His glory. If the reasoning behind your asking isn't His glory, let Jesus back in as the Lord of your life.

Once you've made your list, cross the things off that aren't rooted in His glory. Tweak them toward His glory, and in so doing, allow Him to tweak your heart toward His glory.

LIVE IT

This is the crazy part. He said that He can do more. Obviously. He's God. According to His power. Obviously. He's God. His power that is at work. Obviously. He's God. Within you.

…Oh. Crap.

Stop writing yourself off as an unimportant character in the advancing of God's Kingdom in your town. God isn't looking for people with titles or resources. He wants people that give Him enough room within themselves that He can work powerfully for His glory.

Kill the little things that get in the way of God showing himself powerful in your life. Risk some credibility. Risk some grasp on sanity. Risk some reputation. Live risky so that our generation might be marked by men that are caught in a glory storm, caught in a powerful move of the God who is able to do more.

OWN IT

READ IT

Most of us have heard the Christian creation story. God speaks for five days, creating everything out of nothing. Then, on the sixth day, He takes dirt, forms a man and breathes into his nostrils and he becomes a living being. God takes a rib from this man and creates a woman out of his rib. They live together with God in paradise. They are naked and shameless.

Then Genesis 3 happens. Read it.

Notice a few things:

- Where was the man while the woman was talking to the serpent?

- What questions does God ask?

- What order does He go in (chain of responsibility)?

- What does God do for them after cursing them?

SINK IN IT

Countless stand up comedy bits and Sunday morning comics have been made about Eve eating the apple and how it's her fault that we're all in this mess. We know from the story though that it wasn't necessarily an apple, she wasn't named Eve yet, and in verse 6, we learn that the serpent and the woman were not alone. The man was there the whole time, watching this interaction, passively allowing it, then participating in the fall of the human race.

Then, God asks questions. God knows. God knows where they are, who told them they were naked and that they had eaten from the tree. God asks questions so that humans can wrestle with what is going on inside them. God gives them a chance to own it. But they don't. The man blames the woman, the woman blames the serpent. As if God didn't give them the freedom to choose.

The questions He asks begin when He calls out to the man. The woman ate first, but God holds the man responsible first. It is always easier to blame others for the mess we end up in. Many times they had their hand in it in one way or another. But when it comes down to it, you have the freedom to choose.

There are consequences for sin. God curses them and as He is kicking them out of the garden, He kills an animal to create some better clothing than just some leaf skirts. But more than that, we see that God is still their provider. He is still caring for them. It is the first example for us that when we sin, blood is shed. The atonement (the thing that makes up for the sin) always involves death.

Consider your life and your own blame game. There are sins of commission, where you choose to sin, and there are sins of omission, where you don't do the right thing when you have the chance. Most men swing between passively watching the fall of man, hoping they won't be held responsible, and actively disobeying God, hoping their mental justifications will hold up if ever confronted.

PRAY IT

Let God call you out today. Let Him ask you about your sin. Own the things that you have blamed others for. Take responsibility for every choice you have made regardless of justifications or outside influence. Own it.

Answer the question that God is calling out to you: "Where are you?" What have you been hiding behind? Take some time and answer these. Write them out. Let Him ask the next question and the next question. And answer them. Sink in those answers. Let His questions affect you.

LIVE IT

In the end, there are consequences for sin. But God also deals with you by caring for you, providing for you, and atoning for your sin. Jesus did all of these. He cared for you by showing you how to live. He provided for you by sending the HS to fill you, guide you, comfort you, and remind you of everything He taught. He atoned for you by climbing on a cross, taking your death penalty, and defeating death in the process.

Live aware today. Aware that all day long you will be the target of lies. You have the freedom to choose not to sin. Whether that means quitting the thing that you know you shouldn't do or doing the thing that you know you should do.

Tell at least one person within the next 3 hours about any sins that you have owned up to. Ask them to pray for you. Don't be a pansy. Do it.

THE CROSS

READ IT

There are a lot of verse references today. In a culture like the one we have in America, where the God of the Bible shows up everywhere, you get used to hearing about the cross. Hopefully, you will see the cross in a new light, as part of the whole story.

Look up these verses and write them out in your journal.

- Psalm 5:5

- Hosea 9:15

- Amos 5:21

- Malachi 1:3

- Revelation 2:6

If these were the only verses you had out of the Bible, chances are that you would not conclude that God is love. In fact, even the popular saying "God loves sinners but hates sin" is contradicted by the scriptures listed here.

Look up John 3:16 and add it to your list of scriptures today.

Now, if these were the only verses you had, you might think that these are two separate gods. We have tried to make sense of love and hate by setting them up as opposites, but that is not what is presented to us in the Bible.

SINK IN IT

Sink this in. God loves everyone in the world, and God hates sinners. Can God do both? Of course. He has to.

If God is love.

Real love.

Pure love.

Nothing but love.

The absolute standard of love.

The image of selfless love.

And the creator of all things.

Then anything less than hate toward everything that destroys His creation, hate toward those who abuse His creation, hate toward those who pursue selfishness, and hate toward those who embrace wickedness wouldn't be enough.

Since God's love is so perfect, He must hate everything that compromises His love.

So if God hates sinners and all are sinners, then God hates you. You deserve the wrath of God.

And if God loves the world and you are in the world, then God loves you.

This seems like a paradox that cannot be solved.

It is a human paradox, but God solved it.

God solved it with the cross.

Sink in this. The cross has two sides. Wrath and grace. Hate and love. Jesus takes your sin and your penalty. Jesus makes you new and gives you His righteousness. Does God hate sinners? Obviously. The wrath meant for you was poured out on Jesus on the cross. You deserved the cross, but you didn't get it. The love meant for you was poured out through Jesus on the cross. It wouldn't have been love if some person was able to live perfect and then offered their life as a sacrifice. It was love because it was God himself, putting the Son in your place, and taking the torture, the nails, the separation from God. You didn't deserve the love shown on the cross, but you got it.

PRAY IT

In an O.C. SuperTones song called Louder Than The Mob, Matt sings these lines that help personalize this truth.

> *I know I'm just another Thomas, won't believe until I see the hole in Your hands. // I know I'm just another Judas, kiss Your face while I drive the nails in Your hands.*

> *My sin yells crucify louder than the mob that day. // My sin yells crucify louder than any mouth.*

Today, thank God for hating your wickedness enough to send Jesus. Thank Jesus for hating your wickedness enough to crawl on that cross. Mourn the fact that your sins, each and every selfish act, put Jesus on the cross. Until you let it move past your head and affect your heart, it will never really affect your life.

Celebrate the fact that Jesus has dealt with your sins and that you don't have to own them anymore. He bought them. And in exchange, He has given you the righteousness of God. The old has gone the new has come.

LIVE IT

Live new. Pick up your cross and follow Jesus. Live in the tension of love and hate. Hate everything that reeks of your old life. Seriously. Hate it. Love everything that glorifies Him. Take actual steps away from your old life today. And like an explorer, set out to discover what is hidden in this new life. Chase God through life today. Live new.

LOVE & HATE

READ IT

The cross has shown us the coexistence of love and hate, that these two are not polar opposites. Just to be clear though, hate is a servant of love. Love comes first, and hate follows naturally, always submitting to love.

Read Matthew 22:36-40.

It is very clear that the plans and purposes of God for humans involves embracing His love nature and working love deep into the fabric of our lives. In your old life, you loved based on conditions and circumstances. In your new life, you love God and people. Period.

Well, you should.

Sometimes, circumstances and conditions win out, and love is not our response. In order to shift your heart out of the old and into the new, you need to understand hate.

Read Proverbs 6:16-19.

Surrendering your life to God means loving the things He loves and hating the things He hates. And that has to start in you.

SINK IN IT

In Proverbs, Solomon throws out these 6, no 7, things that God hates. But he doesn't just make a list, he uses parts of the body to demonstrate how personal these things are. It is easy to see these things in other people, but you're going to focus on you.

Your eyes.
Your tongue.
Your hands.
Your heart.
Your feet.
Your mouth.
Your actions.

Each part of your life needs to come into alignment with the love of God. Anything outside of that love deserves and demands hate. Hate the lies that well up in you. Hate the arrogance you experience. Hate the evil that takes shape in your heart. Hate the desire to do wrong. Hate your willingness to bend the truth. Hate your part in stirring up trouble. Hate that your hands, either through actions or inaction, have harmed the innocent.

Hate it. Loathe it. Let it wreck you. Let it ruin you. Do not get comfortable with what God hates. Let it get uncomfortable. Sink in it.

When you feel like moving on, don't. Not yet. Go back and read through Proverbs 6:16-19 again. Feel the weight of the things that God hates in you.

Now. Crucify it. It is your old self.

PRAY IT

In prayer today, tell God explicitly, in detail, about the things that He hates in you. Tell Him your stories. Tell Him about the times that you have let these things get in the way of loving Him. Tell Him about the times that you have let these things get in the way of loving others. Tell Him how painful it is to love some of the things He hates. Tell Him how you don't want to be like this.

Tell Him how you hate it too. Ask for a fresh filling of the HS. Ask to be transformed. Ask for your mind to be renewed. Let Him love you.

LIVE IT

In Donald Miller's book *Searching For God Knows What*, he points out that in war, you shoot the enemy, not the hostage. Applying this to your life as a Christ follower illuminates that you were deceived by the enemy, but God has set you free through Jesus by defeating the enemy on the cross. Going through the reading, sinking, and prayer today teaches you a lot about what has gone on in you, learning to hate the things God hates in you and loving God and people.

Reimagine those that are doing the things that God hates as hostages. They need to be set free. They need to be loved even though they may be actively involved in the things that God hates. Understanding the way that God has worked in you builds the hope that He will do the same for them.

Look for ways to love people and God today, praying against the enemy at every turn. Share the good news through your actions and your words. Yeah, actions and words. Have courage. Speak up. Love God. Love people. Live new.

FOLLOW

READ IT

Most religions have rule followers and rule breakers. If you can muster up enough self control to follow the rules then you are "good," but if you let up at all and break a rule, then you are "bad." Christianity is different. There is a popular phrase stating that Christianity isn't a religion, but a relationship. That is a nice theory, but on some level, Christianity is still a religion. It is a faith/worship system involving a supernatural God and humanity. The difference is that instead of following rules, we follow Jesus.

Read Matthew 4:18-22.

Jesus calls you out. He looks at you in the middle of your everyday, trying to figure things out, and calls your name. He says "Come. Follow me." He doesn't prequalify you based on your upbringing, race, language, accomplishments, financial status, or ability to follow rules. He looks at you and calls you out.

At this point, you can drop your life and follow Him, or you can ignore the invitation. It's up to you. No one can make you do it. No one can make you stop. It's you and Him. First, go. Then, follow.

Read Mark 2:13-17.

When you drop your life and follow, you end up in good company. No other follower of Jesus was picked because of their ability to follow rules. Jesus confronted them in their messy, jacked-up life and said, "Follow me." Every follower of Jesus you meet has recognized that He offers hope so far beyond anything they have found in this life that they've dropped everything to follow Him. The problem has been that with the popularization of the labels "Christian" and "Christianity," people claim these labels that Jesus never even talked about. Jesus asked people to follow Him. As time goes on, people have attempted to appear as if they were following Him, as if Christian were a style. Those aren't the same thing. Don't worry about stigmas associated with the popularized versions of His teachings. Follow Him.

SINK IN IT

At some point in your life, you heard about Jesus. Chances, are that you didn't just drop your life and follow Him. It's harder than that now. Jesus isn't actually standing there asking you to follow Him. However, once you realize that Jesus is real–He really did live a perfect life, die your brutal death with your sins on His back, get buried for three days, was raised from the dead, ascended back into heaven, and sent the HS to guide and comfort you–once you realize that, you also realize that the hard part wasn't whether or not He is physically standing there, it's dropping your life.

Simon (Peter), Andrew, James and John were fisherman. Levi (Matthew) was a tax collector. They had lives, plans, dreams, regrets, questions, and concerns. Jesus shows up and they dropped everything to follow Him. Jesus didn't ask them to pray a prayer to accept Him. Jesus didn't give them four spiritual laws or sixteen articles of faith to memorize. Jesus didn't ask them to go to a small group, or weekend services. Jesus didn't tell them about himself and ask them to come hang out for an hour on Sunday to sing songs to Him.

There is a massive difference between meeting Jesus and then spending the rest of your life talking/studying/singing about Him, and meeting Jesus, dropping your life and following Him.

Take stock of your life. Have you met Jesus, or are you following Him? Think about your last 48 hours. Is Jesus someone you talk about on occasion? Or is Jesus the one constant thing throughout your days. Do you really have a relationship with Him, or is He more like a celebrity that you've met and know a lot of facts about?

Sink in it. Let it affect you. Let it bother you. Don't rush past this. Don't just decide that you're one or the other. Chances are you have had seasons of both. What are you now?

Write some of these thoughts and answers to the questions in this section in your journal.

PRAY IT

Being a follower and regressing into someone who knows a lot of facts but isn't marked by a life of following Jesus sucks. "Followers" that aren't actually following anymore aren't called sort-of followers. They aren't called strugglers or back sliders. They are called deserters.

Chances are that if you've picked up this book, you've experienced this. Much like Peter, you know Jesus, you've even followed Him, but you've also deserted Him.

Tell God what's up. What's going on in your heart and your head right now? Let it out. Feel bad. Feel sorry. Regret your actions. Regret your loss of passion. Regret the promises you've made that you weren't able to keep. Tell God what's up.

LIVE IT

Also like Peter, rest assured that Jesus hasn't abandoned you. Peter denied Him three times (once within ear shot) on the night that He was crucified. In the last chapter of the book of John, Jesus finds Peter and recommissions him. Jesus assures him that what's over is over, and there is too much at stake in what's to come to live there. Jesus essentially tells him to get off his boat (again) and live new. The old is gone. It's ok to hate what happened, but don't linger too long. Linger just long enough to feel how real it is, but don't stay.

Take some sort of physical action to step out of this moment. Put on some shoes. Put on a jacket or a hat. Walk out of wherever you are and find the place where you go all the time—your work, your friend's house, your favorite coffee shop, whatever. Go there and do something that will remind you all the time that you've walked out of your old life. Be creative. Set up a reminder that maybe only you will know about, but will beckon you every day to live new.

SELF CONTROL

READ IT

One of the frustrations of following Christ is desires that don't honor Him. Jesus never said that desires would go away. It's part of life. In Genesis 3, before the fall, the woman desires to eat the fruit for gaining wisdom. Desire happens.

It's like this. Your life is a city. And when you are the king of your city, there are times that you feel in control, and other times where you feel out of control. Regardless of how you feel, you are out of control. There is chaos festering beneath the surface all over the place. As that bubbles up more and more you get to the point where you realize that you suck at being the king of your city. You need someone to save you because everything is broken and being held together by what little strength you have left. In steps Jesus. He ascends the steps of your life, dethrones your ego, and takes the rightful place as the King of your city, the Lord of your life.

When Jesus is King, chaos dies down. Order is established. The undisciplined get discipline. Systems are rebuilt from the ground up. By the time Jesus is done with it, it's a new city. And in this new city, desires have someone that they answer to. It's not that they don't exist. It's just that now there is a King with a backbone that says no to the bad ones and yes to the good ones.

Read Galatians 5:16-25.

SINK IN IT

This passage is very interesting. There are desires that you want and desires that you don't. Then there are 2 lists: the acts or works of the sinful nature or flesh and the fruit of the Spirit. Why didn't he say acts or works of the Spirit? Or fruit of the godly nature? Why was he so specific with the fruits of the Spirit?

Everyone understands fruit. Unless you're a toddler, you know how fruit exists. Fruit grows on trees, bushes, and vines. Seeds are planted and watered. If the sprout receives enough sunlight, water, and nutrients, and is protected from freezes and high winds and is grown at the right altitudes in the right soil, eventually the plant is big enough to bear fruit.

So when he writes "fruit of the Spirit," there is so much more going on than a simple action or work. Fruit is evidence of a lot of environmental work, energy and growth. Good fruit is evidence that the conditions have been right and well for some time.

Love. Joy. Peace. Patience. Kindness. Goodness. Faithfulness. Gentleness. Self-control.

You see these things in the lives of others and it's natural, unforced, and awesome. You might think, "I want fruit of the Spirit like that." But you should say "I want roots like that. I want to live in that soil. I want to be pruned like that. I want to be watered like that."

If you think you have a self-control problem, you have discovered that you have a problem with your connection with the HS. You've got root issues. Soil issues. Sunlight issues. Water issues. Nutrient issues. You've got to get connected to the HS, allowing God to prune you, letting the Word wash over you and water you, letting your roots go down deep in the HS, and after some time, there will be evidence that looks like self-control.

PRAY IT

Ask God about your environment. Are there rocks and weeds in your soil that need to be pulled out? Do you have enough light or are you still living in shadows? Is the Word watering your heart daily or is it just once in a while, and you try to drink it up, but it never lasts? Do you have overgrown areas that need the Gardener to prune some branches back?

Write out some honest environmental issues that could lead to a better root system, a better connection with the HS.

Ask for endurance and perseverance and strength in the storms.

LIVE IT

This is the long haul. Probably, you won't see fruit today. But make sure that Jesus is sitting on the throne, deciding which desires get the yes and which ones the no.

Go find someone that you would say has the fruit of the Spirit. Tell them about the fruit metaphor. Ask them what kind of an environment has helped them develop and maintain a connection with the HS. From that, make at least 2 environmental changes. Tell someone about the changes and ask them to ask you about it everyday for the next week.

ARMOR OF GOD

READ IT

Everyone that thinks Christianity is boring has been lied to and has believed it. You are in the middle of all out war. Boredom isn't a byproduct. Boredom is a weapon of your enemy. The call, provision, and purposes of God are thick with adventure–and your life matters.

Imagine your spiritual commander is pumping you up, getting you ready for battle with epic music building in the background. Read Ephesians 6:10-20.

SINK IN IT

This is what you were built for. It is obvious from this text that war is happening. You are either fighting in it or a casualty of it. When you grow bored with the fight, know that you have been targeted and wounded.

Wake up. Your life matters. God is giving you every piece of armor you need.

Truth holds your pants up. Without it, you're walking around, pulling up your pants all day. In war, you shouldn't have to think about something as trivial as pants, but you are. Your hands are pulling up your waistline instead of holding a sword. Truth is essential. Truth doesn't change. Truth isn't an idea or a position on an idea. Truth is a person. Get to know Him. Otherwise you'll spend your day grasping at things that you wish you could control. Cinch it tight.

Righteousness protects your vital organs. It is your number one defense against attacks. It is not your own. It was given to you in an exchange for your sins when Jesus climbed on the cross. He took everything wrong with you and gave you everything right with Him. It's His righteousness. And it is impenetrable. Don't defend with your righteousness. Defend with His. It cannot be dented or damaged. Where your righteousness falls short, His always stands strong. Put it on.

The gospel moves you. This is the gospel, the good news: you aren't anchored to the creation that is subject to the frustration of decay. This gospel moves you. You are born again, into a spiritual family, and you are now a living embodiment of the good news to everyone you meet. When you encounter how messed up the world is, the gospel moves you to free people from it. God is putting everything back together, making everything new, and it moves you.

Your faith may be small, but it is enough to protect you from every attack. And the attacks will come. Fire arrows that look like minor distractions, that smell like shifts in attitude and fly like unbelievable phone calls. Your enemy works as an embezzler, stealing moments, glances, thoughts, and breaths. One at a time. And over time, he hopes to get an arrow through. He hopes that one will hit home and shake you. You've been given a shield called faith. Learn to use it. Learn how to lean into it when he shoots high and low. Your faith matters. Put it to good use. Don't let him pick you off.

Your head is protected by salvation. It fits right. It hugs in the right places while letting you see and hear everything around you. You are protected. It allows you to respond without worrying. Get comfortable in it. Learn to trust it. He has done everything to secure it. Never take it off. It is now part of who you are. Be thankful, love it and learn to live in it.

Your only physical weapon is the HS, the very Word of God. God has given you an offense. His Word in your heart. The HS is your guide, reminding you of everything that Jesus taught. Get His Word in your heart. It is your only hope at having a positive impact on this war. When you get His Word in you, and it begins reading you more than you are reading it, your enemy is offended. Constantly. Your life becomes offensive to him and His Kingdom, and your life matters in this all out war.

Don't be a casualty of war—wearing boredom like a pair of sweat pants. This is war. Act like it.

PRAY IT

Paul ends this passage around the idea of prayer. Some people like to say things like "All we can do now is pray." Prayer is the atom bomb for Christians. There is nothing more powerful than calling out to the God of the universe. Pray like it depends on God and it gives room for God to move.

So pray. Pray for everyone that God brings to mind. Go to war for people. Pray every scripture you know over the people you encounter, your pastors, your friends and family. Put some spiritual skin in the game. You've got access to the good news and the God that sent it and people that are desperate for it. Act like it. Pray your guts out for people that need to be brought from death to life. Satan will hate you for it. This is what it means to be a Christian. Love with prayer today.

LIVE IT

People want to blame bad events on God. Truth is, almost every bad event basically boils down to some sinner acting like a sinner should. Don't blame the dark for being dark. Blame the light for not being as bright as it should be. Don't look for demons under every rock, but don't think that you're not playing a critical role in this war. God's got ahold of your heart. He redeemed you to put you into work battling for those that are still held hostage by the enemy. Be light today.

PRAYER

READ IT

Psalms were written at real times by real people that weren't afraid to be honest with God and actually hear from God–even if it was hard information.

Psalm 4 is honest, good, rich, promising, and deep. The first verse is a cry out to God. In verse two, God speaks back. He asks three questions. Verses three and four answer the first question. Verse five answers the second question, and verse six answers the third question. Verses seven and eight are the supernatural result of God hearing a prayer and answering it.

Read the chapter a few times. Underline any words or phrases that grab you.

SINK IN IT

Map it out. Get a piece of paper, or use one in your journal. Write out the three questions from God. Depending on your translation, you may need to separate them out. The first is about God putting up with us because we turn glory into shame. The second is asking how long you will want what isn't true. The third (which may look like it is part of the second) is asking how long you will seek false gods and the illusion of their power. Then, line up the answers to the questions from the passage. Spend some time thinking about how these questions are relevant in your life, and what the answers for each question mean for you.

Now go back and read verse one and then verses seven and eight. If you want verse one. If you want verses seven and eight to be true about your life, you've got to get verses two through six deep down in your heart.

Pick a specific part of this chapter and memorize it, asking God to show you deep in your heart what kind of change it will require in your life. Not later. Right now. Spend some time and memorize it.

PRAY IT

Go back to the words and phrases that you underlined and begin to personalize them. Write them out as a prayer in your journal. Include the real details of your life around the emotion, questions, answers, and honesty in the scripture. Insert this psalm into your real time and be real with God as you pray through it.

LIVE IT

Remember that part of the chapter that you memorized. Hit repeat. All day. Tell someone about that part of this chapter and what God is speaking to you about changing. If that change involves other people, make sure to include them. Be relentless about this piece of scripture actually playing out in your life today. In every transition between this thing and that thing today, go over that verse in your head, in your heart and out loud. Invite the HS into the transitions of your day to help, guide and comfort you.

COMFORT

READ IT

One of the lies that Satan tells as people move from old to new life is that life will be more comfortable on this side, after you are born again. This is obviously a lie because Jesus told us that the HS is our guide and comforter. If life was more comfortable as a surrendered Christ follower, we wouldn't need the HS to comfort us.

Plenty of people have bailed on following Jesus because they believed this particular lie. And even if you would never have said that you believed it, we have all experienced times where we think things like "Why me?" or "It wasn't supposed to be like this, so why is it?"

The writer of Hebrews gives good insight into hardship, suffering, trials, and other discomforts of all kinds.

Read Hebrews 12:3-14.

Our subconscious first reaction to anything uncomfortable is to question why. Sometimes we skip right past the why because we are so sure we already know the answer. The writer of Hebrews doesn't try to figure out why, but suggests another way. In verse 7 the idea is that regardless of why, treat this uncomfortable time as discipline from God. Essentially the writer is saying that we should recognize our lack of discipline, and because we understand how good of a Father God is, seek to learn from Him at every uncomfortable turn any lesson that He would teach us.

SINK IN IT

You are reading this in one of two states right now. Either you are uncomfortable and processing this based on your current hardship or you are comfortable and need to learn and remember this for later.

Either way, it starts with considering Jesus. Look to Jesus. Look at His life. Look at His death. Look at His endurance. He is the rock and gives you a focal point so that you won't lose heart. Chances are, nothing you have experienced compares to the brutal torture He endured to save you and glorify God.

This is the big picture, that if God allowed Jesus to go through that and Jesus came out on the other side alive, then there is hope for your situation. As you consider Jesus and your focus moves from your situation to His, you are zooming out and including Truth in a story that was too small. Once you are here, you can begin to ask this question: "What do You want me to learn?"

If you are still asking God "Why?" then you can't really look at what He wants for you. He never promised to give you answers for your discomfort. He never promised that if you followed Him that He would make your life comfortable. He promised that He would be with you.

PRAY IT

Start by writing down your hardships in your journal. Tell Him what has gone on. Tell Him what is so uncomfortable in your heart and in your mind and in your spirit. Tell Him the details about how hard it has been.

Then, write down the story of Jesus' death. Write it down in your own words. (If you don't remember what happened, you can look it up in Mark 15.) Think about how He could have stopped it, but He didn't. He let it happen. All of it.

Now look back and read over your story. Ask God, what do You want me to learn from this? How are You bending me to know You more? As You break me and put me back together, what are You changing in me?

Spend time sitting in this, allowing God to speak to you.

LIVE IT

As life goes on, things will become uncomfortable for a time and comfortable for a time. It will continue on like this for the rest of life here on earth. Learn to react to the uncomfortable seasons with the question, how is God using this to discipline me? You won't come out unscathed. In fact you will probably be injured emotionally and physically, but spiritually you will be refined. Learn to trust God. Run to Him.

And in the comfortable seasons, tell the stories about when it hurt, when it seemed unbearable, how hard it was, and how He never left you. Tell the stories of His faithfulness. People need to be reminded. You need to be reminded. God isn't merely a god of comfort. He is the Living God, Emmanuel, God with us. So in the middle of all the uncomfortable moments, He is with you. Take comfort in that.

EXPERIMENT 10

AUTHORITY

READ IT

When you are young, you are told what to do and what not to do. Typically, if you do what's right, then you are rewarded, but if you do what's wrong, then you are punished. This is the basic pattern of dealing with young children. This continues through adolescence. But something happens as a teenager. You slowly understand what authority is and that you're not in it. In desperate grasps at being your own authority, rebellion takes over, secrets abound, and many parent/child relationships become fractured through this process. Then, as adults, some seek to put themselves in places of authority. Others avoid it at all costs while criticizing those that have it.

Jesus didn't live opposed to authority. Jesus didn't live to climb the authority ladder. Jesus didn't even live as the authority. Jesus lived under authority.

Read Matthew 8:5-13.

Notice how the centurion perfectly explains Jesus' relationship to the Father and how authority works. Jesus wasn't able to perform miracles because He had authority. He was under authority first. Real authority is given.

Read Matthew 28:18-20.

This is one record of the parting words of Jesus to His disciples. After Jesus dies, is buried, and is raised from the dead, all authority in the heavenly realms and throughout the earth was given to Him. With this authority, He commissions His followers to do what He did. He essentially gives them part of the authority that He had been given to do the things that He would do.

SINK IN IT

You are a man under authority. Some of these authorities are placed over you while some of them you have willingly placed yourself under. Every day, you make decisions based on whether or not you will be caught by those in authority over you. When you decide that the likelihood of getting caught is low enough, you risk it and step outside of the boundaries that have been set for you. Chances are that this is never the result of getting up, getting on your face, begging God to be glorified in and through your life, and the HS prompts you to step outside the boundaries. You probably have a lot of reasons for crossing those boundaries. Maybe you think that those boundaries are to keep people safe that are less mature than you. Maybe you think that those in authority don't understand what is a big deal and what isn't a big deal–that if they would get out from behind their desks and actually live life, they would see it your way. Maybe you are stuck outside the boundaries because you are too afraid of the consequences, so you just keep ignoring authority. Maybe you have decided that you're not going to be told how to live your life. Whatever the reasoning, you're wrong.

Aside from those in authority creating boundaries for you that would require you to disobey the commands of God, you are to live under the authorities that God has established. You don't have to. But then you wouldn't be a Christ follower. You would be a self follower. You would be your own authority.

Call it what it is. Rebellion against authority that does not contradict scripture is against Jesus.

But more than that, you're missing the point of living under authority! You are missing the point. Jesus lived under authority and single handedly advanced the Kingdom of heaven forcefully. Then, He is given the authority that He was under and puts you under that authority in the same way that He was!

LIVE IT (SWITCHED WITH PRAY IT TODAY)

You are called and commissioned to live under authority, forcefully advancing the Kingdom of heaven in the same way that Jesus did, not testing the boundaries of authority. Submission to the authority of Christ in your life leads to unbelievable freedom in being a godly man that forcefully advances the Kingdom in your town. Don't waste energy focusing on the boundaries. Embrace the authority that is given to you and use it to do the things that Jesus did, making disciples, baptizing them in the name of the Father and of the Son and of the Holy Spirit, teaching your disciples to obey the things that Jesus has commanded you. He is with you. Act like it.

But before that, you may need to go to those that are in authority over you and confess the ways that you have stepped outside of the boundaries and ask for forgiveness. There may be consequences. That's ok. There should be. You need discipline.

PRAY IT

Just respond to God. Repent for the ways that you have looked at authority the wrong way. Repent for the ways that you have wasted the authority that you are under. Bring every aspect of your life under the authority of Christ. Tell Him about how you have rebelled and followed yourself instead of Him. Tell Him how you are moving from beyond the boundaries back into alignment with the authorities He has placed in your life.

Establish the prayer conversation that will happen as you are presented with options that go beyond the boundaries that He has set for you. Make a list of questions like: Will this glorify You? Does this contradict scripture? Will this advance Your Kingdom? If I did this, would I feel like hiding it from those in authority?

Ask God to show you the freedom that comes by living under the authority of Christ.

BRAVERY

READ IT

Open your Bible to 1 Samuel 14. If you look back a few verses, you will see that the armies of Israel didn't have any weapons except those that belonged to the king Saul, and his son Jonathan. Jonathan doesn't have much. But he has a sword and faith. In one of the most ridiculous stories in the Bible, Jonathan seems to have no sense of military strategy at all.

Read the story in 1 Samuel 14:1-23.

Who do you identify with? Jonathan and his bravery or Saul and his chilling under the pomegranate tree? Which would you rather be?

SINK IN IT

Verse 6 is godly bravery at it's finest. Jonathan doesn't have everything figured out. But he knows something about the character of God and the few resources he has available.

He devises a plan (as ridiculous as ever there was in war), and he goes for it.

Your life is full of moments where you've thought "What if God doesn't move? What if this God thing doesn't work out?"

What if the rest of your life was full of Jonathan-esque moments where you think "What if God does move? What if this God thing does work out?" You've got to ask the right question.

Godly bravery isn't careless. It's careful and cautious. But after the careful, cautious strategy involving the action of God for His purposes is created, bravery is implementation. Bravery is getting up and doing the thing.

Bravery isn't worried about God being weak. Bravery is bringing the few resources you have and letting God be strong in them through action.

And the best part is that Jonathan brings his armor bearer. He tells someone and brings them along. There is something to be said about the accountability of believing God out loud. Bravery doesn't back down when it goes public.

Bravery happens in your heart and your head long before anyone can see the results. Let Him build that in you.

PRAY IT

There are plenty of people that are better positioned, better resourced, more talented, and more equipped than you are. But God is speaking to you about bravery right now.

Talk to Him about the times in your life that you haven't stepped out in godly bravery because you asked the wrong question. Ask Him to show you how big He wanted to be in those moments.

Talk to Him about the things in your immediate future. What might He want you to do so that He can advance the Kingdom through your life with the little resources that you have? Don't be afraid to dream big dreams. Perhaps He will act in your behalf.

LIVE IT

Tell someone. Invite them in. Conspire with them. We have a real enemy that hates you and your friends and everyone in your town. God wants brave men that will step out in faith with the good news that Jesus came to set them free. God wants brave men that will love people that are avoided and marginalized. God wants brave men that will believe He can do great things through ordinary people with barely enough resources in your town.

Don't write anything down for LIVE IT today. Do it.

SEEK FIRST

READ IT

You are going to read words from Jesus today. Jesus often spoke in parables, short stories with deeper meanings. In the first passage, however, Jesus is very straight forward. Jesus calls out the truth that we chase the things that worry us, and He implies that the things that worry us are the valuable things to us. Then He teaches us something about the character of God and tells us plainly what we ought to do.

Read Matthew 6:31-33.

What are the things that you worry about? School? Work? Money? Pleasure? Purpose? Acceptance? Looks? Success? Reputation? Abilities? Possessions? Getting caught?

Before reading the next passage, make a quick list of the things that preoccupy your thinking and you end up chasing.

If we are to seek His Kingdom first, we need to see what that looks like. Jesus gives us three examples of His Kingdom in parables.

Read Matthew 13:24-33.

There are plenty of things in life that aren't wrong or even necessarily bad, but everything that you seek first before God's

Kingdom and His righteousness is settling for less than God's best in your life.

SINK IN IT

In the Matthew 6 passage, Jesus is calling out worrying about things that are necessary for life–food, shelter and health. When He indicates that something will be added after seeking His Kingdom first, He isn't talking about much more than basic provisions.

Do some work, crossing the things off your list that wouldn't matter if you found complete acceptance and provision in God.

Now, pick one of the three parables about the Kingdom that made the most sense for your life. In your journal, write out a short story about how that should look in your life. Maybe you'll write about really big things, like the way that the Kingdom changes your future and your planning. Maybe you'll write about really small things, like what you do when no one is looking.

Write an honest story that makes sense with your life and captures the idea of the parable.

PRAY IT

Ask God about your story. Maybe you wrote a good one. Maybe you couldn't find the words. Ask Him why you ended up with this story.

Now, ask God about your life. If He was going to make any edits, what would those be? God is the master storyteller, the author and perfecter of your faith, and the literal beginning and end. Sit with the master of story and let Him work on your story through prayer.

Maybe there are sections of your life that need to make the cut. Maybe there arc others that aren't necessarily bad, but have come before God and need to be cut. Maybe there are areas that are completely devoid of your heart seeking His Kingdom and need to be completely rewritten. Talk to Him about it.

LIVE IT

Ok. Physical challenge/metaphor. Sit up tall. Push your chest out a little bit. Imagine your heart seeking out what it wants. Picture His Kingdom as an object off to the side of where you are sitting. If His Kingdom is off to the left or right, let your chest turn that direction, slightly but surely. Intentionally. Feel that? There is suddenly direction and purpose, even though not much has changed.

This is how we should seek first His Kingdom. As you enter or sit in situations, ask Him what His Kingdom looks like here, and turn toward it. Turn your attitude. Turn your mind. Turn your heart. Shift your weight. Intentionally move the events in your life toward His Kingdom. This, is the first priority, and the measure of success for everything we do.

Every moment.

Every place.

Every person.

Every reason.

Every thing.

All for His glory.

First.

BOLD

READ IT

In Chapter 3 of Acts, Peter and John are walking into the temple and have an encounter with a beggar. He asks for money, and Peter tells the dude to look at him. Peter tells him that he doesn't have any money, but he has something else to give him. "In the name of Jesus Christ of Nazareth, walk." As if this wasn't enough, Peter reaches down and grabs his right hand and helps him to his feet.

Can you imagine what was going through Peter's mind? He was probably thinking, "Either this is going to be awesome or super embarrassing." Well, it was awesome. The guy gets up and praises God like a gymnast. People are staring, so Peter tells them what's up. This brings us to today's reading.

Read Acts 4:1-13.

SINK IN IT

Sink in this: Peter was the guy that denied Jesus three times on the worst night in the history of the world. Now, he's standing up to the authorities. The priests, the captain of the temple guard and the Sadducees are all blown away by their boldness because they were just ordinary guys. But they took note that they had been with Jesus.

What's the difference? How did Peter the Denier become Peter the Bold? The answer is in verse 8. It wasn't a string of self-help books. He didn't believe in himself. He didn't finish his Masters of Divinity. He didn't climb the ladder of boldness.

He was filled with the HS. He spent time with Jesus and opened himself up enough to let the HS fill him. And he walked in that.

Bold is not the goal. Bold is the byproduct of time with Jesus and being filled with the HS.

PRAY IT

Start off your prayer time today with repenting. Get specific. Name some times when you have been the denier, either literally or by intentionally skipping that detail of your life. Name some times where you should have been hanging out with Jesus but you settled for mindless escapism instead. Name some times when you've been filled with your self instead of His HS. Apologize. On your face. Ask for forgiveness. Don't make any promises. Just sink in the crappy-ness of your sin.

Go to round 2. Ask Him to show you more times that you've relied on your own strength, times you doubted that He would show up, times you considered the HS a last resort, etc.

Apologize. On your face. Ask for forgiveness.

Feel it. Mourn it. Let it out.

As you've done this, you are making room in your heart, in your mind and in your life. Ask God this very simple thing that we so often forget is the most necessary:

God, please fill me with your HS.

LIVE IT

Focus on the other half of repenting today. Repenting starts with confession. The pivot point is the filling of the HS. The result is a life lived in the opposite direction.

Chances are, you aren't a Bible scholar. But you have been learning to spend real time with Jesus, the Word of God. If you went through the prayer exercises, God has promised to pour out His HS in your life.

Categorically, you aren't much different than Peter. Don't be surprised when there are clear moments today where you can glorify Him by stepping into moments for His glory. There will probably be a risk of reputation. There will probably be broken people involved. It probably won't fit nicely into your schedule.

But stepping into those moments is important. God is preparing you now for what He is preparing for you soon. Don't miss the training, life altering, God glorifying opportunities as they present themselves today. Don't seek boldness for boldness sake. But don't be afraid of boldness for God's sake either.

Spend time with Jesus. Be filled with the HS. And let loose.

POWER

READ IT

Power is tricky. Suppose an olympic athlete is approaching the world record for the deadlift. That lift could be described as powerful. Now, suppose you are approaching your personal record for the deadlift and end up setting a new record. To say that your lift wasn't powerful because the other one appears more powerful would be wrong. It still takes power.

Life takes power. God gives you power to live. As you learn to live new, you can surrender the power that He has given you, trading it for the power of the HS. You also have the option of hanging on to your power, but that would be settling.

It's like a circuit set up with a AA battery, a light and a switch. Jesus is described as the light of the world. Then, He tells His followers that they are the light of the world. When you leave your own path, follow Him, and He sets you free and makes you new, He flips the switch. You are a light. The question is, are you going to give up the little power you have in your AA battery to hook it up to the nuclear power plant that is the HS? Both are powerful, but one greatly surpasses the other.

This is a helpful metaphor, but what does that actually look like in real life? Paul writes about the result of this in his second letter to the Corinthians.

Read 2 Corinthians 3:4-18.

The old covenant was glorious, but nothing compared to the new covenant. The face of Moses showed the dripping faucet that was the glory in the law, but the surpassing glory of the life filled with the power of the HS is a glory storm—a torrential downpour.

SINK IN IT

The old life was lived for alternative glory, like glory for the business, glory for the self, glory for the family, glory for the organization, glory for the body, glory for the team, etc. The new life is lived for the glory of the One. The reason God sends the HS is for His glory. The HS has roles of helping you, guiding you and comforting you, but all of those things aren't the end. The end is His glory. That's why this passage on the power of the HS centers around glory. Everything is for His glory, or else it's not powered by Him.

In order to really live this out (everything for His glory) in the present moment, Paul writes about how we have to deal with the past and the future. Once you get those lined up right, the HS can be powerful in you in the present for His glory.

In verse 6, Paul talks about what God has done in your past. He has made you competent. You weren't. But you are now. That has happened. You are new because of what He has done. He has put the HS in you and that makes you competent. "You can do it!" is a nice, positive attitude, but it isn't true. You can't do it. That's why you gave up. That's why He sent the HS. So He can do it through you. You have everything you need because you have Him. Be confident in your competence because He is competent in You. This is your recent past.

In verse 12, he sums up verses 7 through 11 with the idea that you have this hope. Glory that lasts. Glory that surpasses. Glory that doesn't quit. Glory upon glory upon glory. Glory in and through your life. God's glory through you. Hope is your expected future. This isn't wishing. This is hope. You have this hope. You have this expectation for your future that God's glory will not quit, but always, always, always persists. You have this expectation for your future that throughout the inevitable ups and downs of life, that God's glory will pulse. You have this hope that His power will not fail like an old battery. You have this hope that God will not shut down His work in your life. Ever. This is your future.

And it makes you bold. This is your present. Your past was moving from incompetence to competence. Your future is secure in the hope of glory. Stop and sink that in. When these grip your heart, He can be powerful right now.

PRAY IT

You used to live for glory in a million things besides the One that deserves it. Walk through those things with God. Tell Him about your old life. Tell Him about the things you used to live for, the things you used to glorify by spending your time, energy and money to make famous. These are the things that will attempt to divert your life from His glory, so get them out in the light, and ask God how to deal with these things.

Tell God about your reservations with what the Word is saying about your past and future. Do you read these things about your past and wonder if it is true for you? Do you ponder your future and struggle with actually expecting to never be let down by Him? Tell Him what is going on so that He can be King of your present.

LIVE IT

Living by the HS is like being blown by the wind and letting it carry you. There are no formulas. There are no maps. There is no usual. But it does have a beginning, a middle and an end. And there are characteristics about living by the HS that seem consistent.

When living by the HS, the end is obedience. The middle is listening. The beginning is asking. Living between competence and hope is the constant cycle of asking, listening and obedience. Learn to ask. Not daily or weekly, but moment by moment. Learn to listen. He will never lead you to do something contrary to the Word of God. Get the Word in your heart so that as you listen you know His voice. He will teach you, guide you and when He does lead you, don't talk yourself out of it. Often, we say we want to do what God wants, then when we hear it and feel it, we talk ourselves out of it. Don't. He has made you competent, and your hope is His glory. Be obedient. When you follow Him, the results are up to Him. It may not have the results you were thinking should happen, but the good result is your obedience for His glory. Live in that.

EXPERIMENT 15

SEXUALITY

READ IT

As we go through life, we form opinions, develop ideas, and grasp certain concepts. This is typically called learning. We receive some information either from someone else that is teaching us or some life experience. Then we form opinions based on the information presented, the style in which it is presented, and this is all based on prior experiences, thoughts and opinions. From there, we develop our own ideas because our minds were created with imagination. We take what is presented to us and decide how that will affect and shape us. Then, as we grasp these concepts, there are some that we hold on to with no intention of ever letting go.

That said...

We are created as sexual beings. Because it is such an awkward topic, most of us have very little information presented to us beyond basic biology as we grow up. The sexuality conversation quickly becomes about preferences. Do you prefer to be sexually active or not? Do you prefer sex with men, women or both? Do you prefer sex with many or just one? Do you prefer a marriage covenant with your sexual activity? Do you prefer to practice sex with yourself when sex with another person isn't an option? Do you prefer sex that is good for you or the other person? Do you prefer sex with love and emotion or sex that is meaningless?

This is a very dangerous road because starting somewhere following childhood, based on biology alone, desires develop. But Satan, in his hatred toward you, has lied to you over and over, preying on your experiences to steal the desire that you as a man should have for his wife and twist it into evil desires.

Read James 1:13-17.

God gives good gifts, perfect gifts. God doesn't change. God doesn't look different in this light or that light. He is light. He wants to speak truth to you where you have bought lies. He wants to give you truth beyond the information and experiences you have used to form opinions, ideas and concepts. He wants you to lay down what you have figured out about yourself, your preferences, and your life. If Jesus is going to be Lord of your life, He gets your sex life too. Let truth reign over the lies of your old life.

SINK IN IT

Sex isn't a preference. You don't get to decide what sex is going to be for you. You gave up that right when you decided that Jesus was going to be the Lord of your life. Sex was created by God and is true and right. Sex beyond the boundaries that God has created is a perversion, it is sin, and it is tied directly to the desires that Satan has perverted in you. Your old life had an idea of what sex should be based on what you had learned about yourself, following your desires. Not anymore.

James tells you that there is a road. Satan laid the road out by lying to you. He has done everything he can to create evil desires in you. For you to say that every desire in you is pure and holy and honoring to God would be ignoring the truth. Satan has paved a road for you with evil desire.

Now that there is a road that is paved for you, he prowls around, whispering temptations that feed off of every lie he has told you. The road is marked out: desire > temptation > enticed > conception > sin > growth of sin > death. Satan isn't going to dangle death out in front of you, but that is his goal. The way that James paints this picture is that there is a moment when desire, temptation and enticement come together to create this perfect storm that he calls conception. You know what this is like. There is a moment in the middle of Satan attacking you where you are sure that you've lost even though you haven't done anything. You know that there is no turning back. It's going to happen.

It doesn't have to. You can say no. But it starts with admitting that there are desires in you that are evil, desires that do not honor God and are not part of your new life in Him. It's weird because it feels like some of these desires are so part of who you are that you can't imagine that this wasn't the way that God made you. Remember that you were born into sin and there are things in you from the very beginning that are not part of your new life. Jesus came to save you from everything that doesn't honor God. That is who you were.

You need to be changed at the desire level. Temptation only works if you desire it. That's why Satan has worked so hard to pervert your desires, so he can tempt you, entice you and ultimately kill you. You need new desires. Biblically speaking, God has designed and created humans as sexual beings, made to enjoy sex in marriage between a man and a woman. If your desires (which are illuminated by the ways that you are tempted) are outside of this, you need new desires. And you're not alone. Think about the ways that you are tempted and work backward. These are the desires that do not honor God and need to be submitted to Jesus as Lord of your life. He gets all of you. He gets to change you.

PRAY IT

Submit your desires to God. Tell Him what they are. Tell Him what you want. Get everything out in the light. Tell Him about why. Tell Him about the experiences you've had and the things you have thought about yourself. Tell Him that you don't want to be tempted by these things. Ask for Him to change you. Ask Him to change your desires.

Explore these questions: How do you desire God? How do you desire to honor God? How do you desire to serve God? When it comes to your preferences in life, do you prefer Jesus?

Don't stop praying. This isn't a one and done. Prayer and the truth in the Word are your two greatest weapons against the desires that you know are lingering from your old life.

LIVE IT

Living in the light and removing the fake power that Satan has over you is how you come alive out of these old desires. There is incredible freedom in saying to another godly man, this is the way that Satan perverted my sexual desires, but that's not me anymore. Find someone and tell them how dark it was back there on that road. Do not allow Satan room to tempt you. Bring it in to the light so that you don't go back down that road. Christ has set you free and your willingness to get real, embarrassing as it may be, is going to show the world that it is no longer you calling the shots, but Christ in you.

Maybe there are situations you are in where you are being sexually disobedient. Because of the nature of sex, there probably aren't a lot of people that know about it. It has to stop. It has to be confessed. Tell someone that is not in the situation. There will probably be consequences. It will probably hurt people. (It actually probably already is hurting people, they just don't know it yet.) Something has to change. Be a man. Do the right thing no matter how hard it is.

If you find yourself being tempted, pray and quote scripture. Replace the desires that surrounded your self with desires that surround your God. Do not combat temptation with your strength. Combat it with the blood of Jesus that sets you free, changes your heart, and gives you life. You're not a spiritually dead slave to sin. You are a redeemed child of God. You are not who you were. You are new. Live new.

RESPONSIBILITY

READ IT

Responsibility is taking psychological ownership for the things that you know you should do or the things that you say you will do. Irresponsibility is denying psychological ownership. Mixed in between these two are guilt and blame. Today, focus on responsibility in terms of what has not yet happened, owning your role in future situations.

You should take psychological ownership of certain things. There are things in living new that you should own. These things become your responsibility. They are a part of the new you. As an owner, you do everything you can to make sure it doesn't fail. You endure late nights. You settle for less compensation. You manage through more stress. You look at the big picture and take small steps toward the vision. You take responsibility.

Read 2 Corinthians 5:11-21 in three different versions. (If you don't have multiple versions, check out youversion.com) As you read, write down words and phrases in your journal that stick out to you. There will be a lot. That's ok. Take a long time on the reading today.

SINK IN IT

So much to sink in. Hopefully a lot sunk in by the third time through.

He isn't sending angels to tell people about Jesus like the shepherds outside Bethlehem. He is sending us. He is sending you. He made you new, not so that you could feel good about yourself or finally feel unguilty or feel clean. He cleaned you and put the HS in you for the sake of others.

Satan would love to keep you in a spot where all you do is work on your relationship with God. Satan wants you to think that the Bible is for you, that church is for you, that prayer is for you, that Jesus is for you. All those things are true, but it isn't the end. Satan uses the Truth, but he twists it and tweaks it to limit the damage to his work. The truth is that all those things are used by God to attain, maintain and build your relationship with Him, but the end is His glory through you for others.

Christ was here for others. He made you new for the sake of others. Sink in that. You have a responsibility.

PRAY IT

Own it. Go over your list in your journal of words and phrases that stuck out to you and take responsibility for the things that God is giving you. Be an owner. Thank Him for trusting you with these things. Tell Him that you are owning it. Tell Him which things you are receiving. He is giving all sorts of stuff in this passage. What things are you receiving? What things are you owning? What things are you responsible for from now on?

LIVE IT

Tell people. You are for them. Let them know. Let them know that you weren't for them, but God has made you new. Do it. Allow the things that Christ has done in you and for you, compel you. Change the way you treat others. Be for them. Be honest. Be trustworthy. Be faithful. Be reconciled. Be responsible. Be new.

VIOLENCE

READ IT

The twelve disciples hung out with Jesus close to every day for three years. That's a lot of time. You could really get to know someone in that amount of time. Jesus has sayings that have become famous like "love your enemy" and "turn the other cheek." You would think that after three years of following Jesus (literally) that they would be doing the things they taught. But the night when Jesus gets arrested, there is some violence that goes down. The interesting part is the beginning and the end.

Read Luke 22:35-53.

It starts off with Jesus asking them to bring swords. This seems different than the message He had been preaching. What happens in the garden is significant in a ton of ways, but probably the best insight is the humanity of Jesus. The simple order of events is something like this:

1. It's about to go down.

2. Got 2 swords.

3. Let's roll.

4. Jesus prays.

5. Disciples sleep.

6. Crowd comes.

7. Judas kisses.

8. Disciples ask, "Swords now?"

9. One disciple goes for it.

10. Ear off.

11. Jesus says "No more."

12. Ear on.

13. Jesus calls them out.

14. And... scene.

Between steps 2 and 11, something changes in Jesus. He goes from wanting to arm His entourage to telling them to stop. Really, the only thing Jesus does between 2 and 11 of any significance is the fact that He prays. It isn't just significant that He prays, but what He prays. Go back and read His words and write them in your journal.

SINK IN IT

It's mind boggling. It is easier to think that Jesus was holy and perfect so He must not have struggled the same way that we do. He did. He even went as far as making plans to protect His life. Jesus had a will contrary to that of the Father. Jesus wanted to save His own skin even though He knew from the beginning that the cross would be the death of Him. But Jesus submitted His will to the Father before acting on it. He asked God to change the game, but quickly realized how selfish that would be. He went for whatever God wanted instead of the selfish plans that were stirred up in His human heart. He submitted every violent thought to God.

He didn't even hide His human nature. He wasn't ashamed of the fact that He wanted something other than what the Father wanted. It's part of being human. He said to bring swords and then told them not to use them. Later, after He had come back to life, someone probably asked Him, "Why did you ask us to bring swords and then as soon as we had a chance to use them you told us not to? What's up with that?" And Jesus didn't hide from it. He was praying all alone, so He could have made something up to save face. But He didn't. He owned up to the fact that He wanted something that God didn't want. He wanted them to bring swords. He sought God. God said no. God reminded Jesus who He was and why He was there. It wasn't to fight. It was to lay down His life for the sake of others. It was for love.

This gets complicated because violence seems like it solves problems. It doesn't. God does. Going to God and asking Him what He is up to and telling Him how hard these circumstances are and asking Him to remind you of who you are and what He has for you to do solves problems. Violence short circuits what God is doing in you and others. Violence ignores God.

You aren't always going to think godly thoughts and make godly plans. But you have to always talk to Him and remember, not your will, but His. Always. No matter how hard. Even if it means the death of you. He can do more with your surrendered, obedient heart than your seemingly justified actions.

PRAY IT

So do it. Talk to God about what pisses you off. Tell Him what makes you feel violent. What makes you angry? What makes you clench your fist and tell your friends to "grab their swords?" Tell Him about your will. Tell Him about how hard it is to do the right thing. Spill everything. Tell Him what you want to do to them. Tell Him.

Then tell Him, "Not my will, but Yours." Let Him bend you. Let Him change you. Let Him win. Let Him teach you about the big picture. Let Him enlighten you. Let Him handle it.

LIVE IT

Breathe. Feel your breath go in and out. He knows. He knows how hard it is to not take matters into your own hands. He knows how hard it is to lay down your life, your will and your actions to let Him be in charge. But this is living out "Jesus is Lord." He's gone through it. He has wanted what God didn't want and walked away from those plans. He's had to tell His friends that there has been a change of plans. He knows. He knows that there is another way.   God will make sure that justice is served. He will. Let Him. Let Him be God.

And remember that it isn't always fight or flight.   There is another way. Jesus didn't run or swing. He let it happen and taught an entire planet about what real love looks like. Sometimes you need to run.   In any sort of an abusive situation, get out.   But leave getting even to God. It is an entirely different way of living. That's why it's called living new.

COVETING, ENVY & JEALOUSY

READ IT

Today you will read about the ten commandments. Most people have some set of rules by which they live their lives. Most people have also heard about the ten commandments. Most people see the ten commandments as an option in deciding where to set the moral standard in their life. Most people see them as a set of rules within a religious system. In other words, if I follow these rules, then I get a gold star, or a crown, or some sort of reward.

In Exodus 19:3-6, we see that the ten commandments are actually part of the covenant that God has with His people. Essentially, He says "I will be your God and you will be my people. Since I am holy and you aren't, we're going to have to set up some sort of guidelines and boundaries for this covenant." So really, the reward is the relationship with God. It makes sense. In a marriage covenant you set up boundaries because otherwise the marriage wouldn't really mean anything.

Read Exodus 20:1-17.

There are some obvious categories in these commandments. The first four commandments all deal with your relationship to God. These are the guidelines for maintaining the relationship. He is first. You don't make any idols. You don't misuse God's name. You take a day a week off from work and rest in God.

Commandments five through nine are all about your relationships with others. Lying. Stealing. Adultery. Murder. Dishonor. All of these are externally observable commandments. You could get caught doing all five of these things. No sane person would want these things done to them, and it makes sense that maintaining a relationship with others is part of God's covenant. He created all of us and wants us to treat each other the way we would treat Him. Love God. Love people.

The final command is different. It isn't really about God. It references other people, specifically their belongings. But it is really about you. Don't covet. Don't want what doesn't belong to you. Don't want someone else's life. This is not externally observable. It is the only command that deals only with your heart and mind rather than your will. If coveting is taken too far, then you end up as a thief, an adulterer, a murderer, an idolater, etc. But no one knows when you covet. Only you know if your motivation is to get what belongs to someone else.

SINK IN IT

Coveting has two sides—jealousy and envy. Jealousy is wishing you had what others have. Envy is wishing that they didn't even have it. Both are forbidden and almost uncontrollable.

There's a line in a movie called *Empire Records* where a store employee named Lucas has stolen $9,000 and gambled it away in an effort to save the store. The store owner Joe is trying to figure out how to come up with the money to fix the problem. Lucas says, "Joe, I think it's going to be ok." Joe asks, "What makes you think that?" And Lucas tells him, "Who knows where thoughts come from? They just appear."

Often, that's what it feels like. You don't know why or where it came from, but all of a sudden, you don't want what you have. Instead, you want what they have. And not just possessions. You want their job. You want their looks. You want their discipline. You want their gifts. You want their talents. You want their courage. You want their relationship with God.

This is why. This is where it came from. There are essentially two commands–love God and love people. Real love is selfless. Real love is laying down your life for the sake of others. So the commands are to lay down your life for God, giving Him praise and honor and glory and worship, and to lay down your life for others, asking not what you can get from them but what you could do for them. The commands are to be for God and for others. When your heart strays from these two primary goals, it instantly turns inward. It is the gravity of fallen man. You want what others have because you have turned the power of love off of God and others and onto yourself.

PRAY IT

Be honest with God. He knows already anyway. Admit to Him the things that you have coveted. Be specific. What are the things that you have been jealous of–things that you wish you could have? What are the things that you have been envious of–things that you wish that they didn't even have?

Talk to God about the four aspects of loving Him and the five aspects of loving others. Which are the hardest parts for you? Where do you need help? Where could God show Himself strong in your weakness?

LIVE IT

Find another guy that loves God and tell him about your heart today. Tell him about the things that you have coveted. Secrets keep you sick. Living in the light as He is in the light gives us fellowship with one another. Ask the other guy to pray for you and commit to telling him again if you find yourself turning love inward instead of outward in the future.

Then, find something to do today, just for God to show Him that you love Him. No one needs to know what it is; it can be just between the two of you. Also, find something to do today to show others that you love them. Do this everyday. As you work these habits into your life, you will find that over time, you won't want anyone else's life.

WASHED

READ IT

Paul is writing a loving, generous left hook to the church in Corinth. They needed to be told plainly to stop.

Read 1 Corinthians 6:9-11 now.

Belief is a choice. We hear a lot of information throughout life, and we choose which of those things we will believe. There isn't a lot of measurable evidence when someone believes in Jesus because not a lot happens. However, there is a ton of measurable evidence (mainly massive changes in behaviors, desires, and reactions) when someone believes that Jesus is Lord. This is surrendering. Believing is different than surrendering.

Paul is trying to teach them the difference here by illuminating three events that happened when a life is surrendered to Jesus.

Verse 9 asks a really tough question. It implies that once you surrender to Jesus, you become a rightdoer, not a wrongdoer.

Then there is the list. Everything on this list is an issue of identity. Satan's lie in this will be "This is who you are." Verse 11 gives the true rebuttal to that lie: "This is who you were."

Then there are the three events—washed, sanctified, justified.

SINK IN IT

Start off by copying the list into your journal. Add to it any ungodly behaviors, desires, and reactions that have crept their way into your identity.

Then, note who does the washing, justifying and sanctifying. It's the HS in the name of Jesus. Note who is the passive agent. You are. When you surrender your life to Jesus, the HS takes over in His name and washes you, sanctifies you, and justifies you. You? You just take it. Like a man.

Read through the "sometimes" listed below and let these three truths sink in.

Sometimes, we feel like we have to scrub the filth out. We feel like surrendering isn't enough. The filth needs to be scrubbed out. But that's not your job. Let the HS wash you.

Sometimes, we settle for thinking that sanctification (being pure and free of sin) is impossible. But this scripture is pretty clear that the HS has the power to sanctify you. Your surrendered life is now pure and free of sin. You don't have to sin anymore because the HS has done a work in you, not because you were able to fix yourself.

Sometimes, we think we need to justify ourselves. Once again, that's not your job. We need to position ourselves under Jesus, the Lord of our lives, and the HS will justify us in His name. That's so hard to do. We've spent our whole lives deciding whether to do this thing or that thing based on the reliability of our justifications for those actions. When Jesus is Lord, He directs, we act, and the justifications are up to Him. That isn't a liberty to have your way as you see fit with your life, but giving the liberty to Jesus to have His way as He sees fit with your life. Because it's not your life anymore. It's His.

The list? Read it out loud. That's not your identity anymore. Your identity is His. Say it out loud.

That's what I was, but You, Jesus, washed me, sanctified me and justified me.

PRAY IT

That was a lot. Pray through the things that have stuck out to you. Talk to God about the things that you're not sure about. Talk to God about what it would be like to look back a decade from now and have confidence that you were washed, sanctified and justified, and that those things on the list really describe who you used to be. Give Him time to speak back. Invite the Word of God to speak over you, reach into the deep parts of your heart and wash you, sanctify you, and justify you.

Sink in it. Don't get up too early.

LIVE IT

Today, own your ex's. Maybe you are an ex-slanderer, an ex-thief, an ex-abuser, an ex-user, or an ex-drunkard. Because this isn't an issue of identity anymore, tell someone. Get it out. Live in your new identity in Christ.

(Satan's only power here is the illusion of power that he holds in secrets. It isn't real power, but he will lie to try to keep you from outing the work of God in you. Secrets are his last grasp at Christ followers. Be a man of God. Walk in the light.)

If you're not who you were, then you can be who you've never been. It's a brand new day.

CELEBRATE

READ IT

The Israelites were God's chosen people. God promised a guy named Abram that He was going to make him into a great nation. God changed his name to Abraham. Abraham had Isaac. Isaac had Jacob. God changed Jacob's name to Israel. Israel had twelve sons. These became the twelve tribes of Israel. They became slaves in Egypt. God delivered them out of Egypt. He was taking them to the land that He had promised to Abraham so many years before. But on the way, they were learning about God in the desert between Egypt and the promised land.

Read Numbers 9:1-14.

Weird, right? They had to eat lamb, unleavened bread and bitter herbs. It would be easy to read over this and think nothing of it. It's just part of a big story that doesn't really have a ton of significance for how we live now. But then that would be reading the story instead of letting the story read you. This is your life.

SINK IN IT

God chose you. You were a slave, but God chose you before you were a slave. You were a slave to sin, and God made a way out for you. He delivered you. He is leading you to the place

He has prepared for you. He could have killed you. He should have killed you. You deserve death for the things you have done. You have sinned against a holy God. Your best deeds are garbage to Him. Your compensation for your sin is death. You deserved a cross. Jesus crawled on it for you, parted the waters at the dead end and made a way for you. The angel passed over. The angel of death didn't destroy you. You didn't get what you deserved. God, in His infinite mercy, spared you.

But He didn't just give you a second try. He didn't set you free and let you fend for yourself. He is leading you into life. Real life. Abundant life. Life that doesn't quit. He is showing you the way.

And in this passage, He reminds you of where you were and what He has done. He has spared you. He has delivered you. And He tells you to celebrate it. Celebrate the fact that He has delivered you from slavery to the promised land. If you are anything like the Israelites, you will ask questions and scream statements that focus on your circumstances. For instance:

"Did you bring me out here to die?"

"Am I really delivered?"

"I'm in the middle of a freaking desert!"

"It doesn't feel like I'm delivered!"

This passage is the second year in the desert. You may be the good part of 40 years away from the promised land and in the middle of the freaking desert, and God says "Celebrate it."

PRAY IT

Tell God your story. Remind yourself. Write it down. Tell Him about your slavery to sin. Tell Him about the moment that you realized that you would never be able to get out. Tell Him about when you gave up trying to save yourself and put your hope and faith in Jesus instead. Tell Him what it was like to be delivered, to be spared, to know that Jesus took the cross that you deserved. Tell Him how uncertain you have been out here in this desert. Tell Him how sure you are that there is a promised land. Tell Him how much you long for the day when the desert is done. Thank Him for delivering you.

LIVE IT

Celebrate it. Do not let your circumstances allow you to lose sight of your past, your God and your hope. Jesus has reoriented your heart. Celebrate it. Set aside time today to celebrate what God has done and is doing in your life. Tell some people. Celebrate with them. Remind each other that He has done and is doing more than you will ever know. Celebrate His love. Remember Him in the middle of the desert.

MONEY

READ IT

The basic biblical financial discipline is the tithe. The basic idea is that you show God that you are grateful for His provision and trust Him as your security and your provider by giving back ten percent. Money isn't necessarily evil. You will encounter money and can use it in ways that honor God. But if you aren't careful and purposeful with how you manage money, you can end up serving and worshipping money rather than God. Giving God back the first ten percent of the money that He provides for you helps keep you managing money on purpose. This first passage is a warning about what happens when you aren't careful.

Read Matthew 6:19-24.

You are on the look out for things you might want in the future. Make sure those things are things that will last—godliness, holiness, faith, integrity, character, influence, legacy, etc. How do you get those things? Not by acquiring more money. You move things from your eyes to your heart. If those aren't the best things, you are darkening your heart.

Much of the Old Testament is a cycle where the Israelites want God and seek God, and then they turn toward something or someone else, darkening their hearts. In the second passage, God is calling them back and telling them how to get back.

Read Malachi 3:7-18.

This is the only place in the Bible where it says to test God. Give to Him by bringing your whole tithe to His house, your local church. See if He won't throw open the floodgates of heaven. They talk amongst themselves and decide to trust God again with income. They trust God enough to live on less. They are convinced that God can do more with 90% of what they have than they could have done with 100% of it. And God finishes the passage by saying that this is significant enough to show the difference between the righteous and the wicked.

SINK IN IT

Money has a way of taking over your heart. When you don't tell your money what's up, it starts to tell you what's up. It's easy to say that giving your tithe to your local church isn't that big of a deal or a hundred other excuses. The only problem with that is the Bible.

God says that you've robbed Him.

God says that those that don't tithe are distinctly wicked.

Ouch.

So if Satan wants you to not serve God, all he has to do is convince you to hold onto your money rather than offer it back to God as a sacrifice. Slowly (and sometimes quickly) but surely, you trust money instead of God. When money isn't there, it is freak out time. Your heart is dark. You've been lied to.

Sink in the truth. Everything is God's. He asks you to give back 10% and even offerings on top of that so that it costs you something. He promises that if you test Him and trust Him, He will pour out blessings. Those may or may not be monetary. If you're not trusting Him with the money He has given to you, what are you so afraid of?

PRAY IT

Today, pray with your palms up. Start with your hands closed like fists, and as you pray, slowly open them. Pray through your thoughts and feelings related to money. Tell God about the times that you've trusted in money rather than Him. Tell Him about how you want your heart to belong to Him, not your bills. Tell Him about how you freak out when you see commas and zeros. Ask Him to show you the way to Him. Ask Him to take you there.

LIVE IT

Lots of people throw out arguments like "The church just wants my money" or "What if they don't spend it right?" The leaders of the local church where you attend are accountable for what is given to them, and you are accountable for what is given to you. But the real problem here is reverting back to the idea that it is your money. It's not. It's God's to begin with. Jesus' plan for spreading the good news is the church. If Jesus is The Lord of your life, support His mission. Building your kingdom isn't an option anymore. It's about the Kingdom. Start with the tithe and set a goal for more. Believe in what God is doing in your town through His church. Set a goal that looks like writing the biggest check every month to the church. If the church, the body of Christ, really is the hope of the world, there is no better investment.

DO

READ IT

Living new isn't all heart, and it isn't all believing. Living new isn't about feeling less guilty or more godly. Living new starts with surrender to Jesus as Lord, He conquers your heart and invades your beliefs, but it ends with you living. Really living. Going out and doing the things that He would do with His heart and mind. This is living new.

Read Romans 10:9-13.

You believe with your heart. You came to the point where you realized that you needed a savior. You've tried to save yourself. You have attempted to be your own savior. You have tried to put your hope in other humans. Every savior is insufficient until you meet Jesus and put your hope in Him. He is the one who saves.

And so you connect your heart to your mind and it results in words. Your words change from "I can fix this. I can figure this out." to "I can't fix this. I can't figure this out. Jesus, save me. Be the Lord of my life." He saves you. He fixes you. He figures it out. He changes your old to new. He takes your heart of stone and gives you a heart of flesh. There is no difference between you and people that seem more godly because they have more rules figured out. We are all justified based on what goes on in our hearts. He has poured out His love on you. He has changed you. You are new.

And He is not done.

Read Romans 10:14-15.

Somehow, you found out about Jesus. That's because someone heard about Him, believed in Him, called on Him to save them, was sent by Him to you, and preached to you. Maybe it was straight up preaching, or maybe it was more gradual (but obviously Jesus). Either way, this story got you to Him. Now you're on the other side. Now you've got something to do.

SINK IN IT

Jesus came back to earth. He did what needed to be done. Then He went back to heaven and sat down at the right hand of God where He intercedes for us everyday. He sent the HS to guide us, comfort us and remind us of everything He taught. But He isn't walking around on earth anymore.

His church planting strategy was to show a group of people how to live by living with them, dealing with their sin so that they wouldn't have to, sending the HS to guide them, setting them free from the old life while giving them a new one, and sending them out to do the same. That has worked. Because now you know Him.

Think about the thousands and thousands of people that may have heard about Jesus, surrendered to Him, and preached the good news that He makes us new. If you could trace the line from you back through history to Jesus, what a story that would be. Suppose this person almost didn't preach Jesus to that person, but the HS nudged and nudged, so the chain wasn't broken and you got to hear. How grateful are you for the HS, for the obedience of that person?

Sink in the fact that you are a link to countless others, not just people that you know, but people that they know and they know and they know...

Your obedience to do the things Jesus did and preach the good news to those trapped in their old lives has exponential potential. Your disobedience has the same exponential potential. If you believe in your heart and confess with your mouth that Jesus is Lord but don't actually do something with that, you've robbed people of saving grace, not just people you know, but people they know and they know and they know...

You're in the middle of a BIG story. Unbelievably big. And what you do matters more than you could ever know on this side.

PRAY IT

In verses 14 and 15, depending on the version you read, it probably uses some verbs like hear, call, send, believe, and preach. Most of those verbs are talking about the next believer in the chain, in the Church. Send is what God does. There is only one that pertains to you now, which is this: preach.

Talk to God about this. What are you afraid of? What have your excuses been in the past? Does it break your heart that people in your life are settling for relationships with people when they could know their Creator–the Savior of heaven and earth? Why or why not? Ask God for His heart. Ask God to know who He has put in your life so that you could introduce them to Jesus. Ask God for courage, boldness, and the power of the HS.

LIVE IT

You're not alone in this. There are millions of other God fearing Christ followers that are responding to this same call today. They have heard the sending whisper of the HS and have stepped out boldly to be Jesus and share Jesus to the people they encounter throughout the day. Take heart. You are not alone. There are a lot of people doing this right along with you.

But also understand this, you don't need anyone else. If it was just you in your town, you could do it. If it was just you in this world, you could do it. If you were the only one that knew that Jesus' cross makes us good with God, that there is grace for the sinner, and that He wants a real relationship with everyone, then the movement of God would not be stopped. You have the potential for the entire movement in you. It started with some guys that met Jesus, got made new, and told the world about who He is. And they were able to do it because of the HS. He is behind all of this. He is working in and through you. You have to be obedient. There is a world of people wishing and hoping for a way out that need you to be obedient. You're not alone in this. The HS is with you, to guide you, comfort you and carry you along.

So go. Preach. Do.

SUCCESS

READ IT

There is a distinct difference between the curse that God put on men and women. We were made different, but we also have different sin natures. There are different consequences for our sin.

Read Genesis 3:17-19.

The first part of verse 17 is God explaining why the curse is about to happen. God reminds Adam that He had commanded him not to eat from the tree, but he listened to his wife instead of God. God is reminding Adam that there is one informer, God. You don't decide for yourself what is right and true. The people around you don't decide what is right and true. God does. And He alone should inform the way you live. He does command you to listen to others (especially those in authority over you), so His informing of your life does include listening to others. But God didn't say to Adam, "Do what your wife tells you to do." So here we are.

Before the woman, before the fall, in Genesis 2:15, God tells Adam to work the garden and take care of it. God is providing food, water, and air along with His presence which feels like love, acceptance, and completeness. Work was there before the fall. But now, God curses. First, God curses the ground.

There will still be provision. Man will still eat. Man will still work. But now there is pain involved. Work will be frustrating. Work will stick you like thorn bushes. There is now a connection between the work that you do and the provision that was there from the beginning. And in the end, the work you do doesn't actually accomplish much for you because you're going back to the dirt. God creates a hopeless cycle for man where the only hope is finding success outside of the cycle, finding hope in God. But the gravity of the cycle will pull you back emotionally, mentally, and physically.

Read Colossians 3:23-24.

There is a way out. It is orienting your emotional success, your mental success, and your physical success in serving God, not your work. In the fall, your heart gets sucked into finding success in your work, but success is always empty outside of serving God.

SINK IN IT

God had provided love, acceptance and completeness, but now we look for those things in what we are able to produce. Success has become this illusion that we chase, connecting our creative abilities with our worth and value. Success doesn't complete. It promises and doesn't deliver. It's like a leaky balloon. Air is pumped in as work is done until it is finished and inflated. But it won't tie off. It won't stay that way. Success puffs up and leaks away. You could spend all of your energy and in the end feel entirely unsuccessful. Success is an illusion. God isn't. Don't chase success. Chase God.

The hard part here is that it is a cycle. You work. You're compensated. You buy. You eat. You work. Etc. And there are these times where you feel like the end of this project or that thing or this vacation is going to make the work worth it. But it doesn't go away. You just keep working. People with millions of dollars keep working. Success is a cycle that will suck you in.

Whether or not you've ever said it out loud, you want success more than God. It's part of the fall. It's part of your sin nature. The gravity of the cycle will pull at you, telling you to put your hope in success rather than in God. You may have even sought God to give you success. It is vicious. It wants to rob you. It wants to ruin you. It wants to set you up and let you down. It wants your heart.

God, however, is relentless. He knew what He would have to do to get you back. He has chased you down and pulled you out. He has given you a new heart. He has opened your eyes. He has given you an out. He has given you another option. You've still got to work. But the end game is different. You no longer look forward to the payoff, the reward, or the successful end. You look at God. You work. But God is what completes you. Finishing your work doesn't complete you. Your work is never done. God completes you. Work for Him, and it changes everything.

PRAY IT

Tell God how you feel. Apologize for the times that you've asked for His hand to move in giving you success in your work instead of asking to know Him. Tell Him about how you have let so many other people inform you on your value (including yourself). Tell Him about how you feel when you are successful and when you aren't successful. Admit that it has been an illusion, that the feeling you strive for or get in success never lasts. Ask God for real acceptance. Ask God for real love. Ask God for real fulfillment. And accept that you will work and work till the day you die, but that work will never fulfill you, God will.

LIVE IT

Serving God is like being a really good waiter at a restaurant. Really good waiters know their customers well. They can tell when they need something before they ever ask. If your aim is to please God while you work and live, then you have to be paying attention to what He wants, what is going on with Him. What is God doing? How can you step in and help that happen? Work diligently with character and integrity. Do everything you can to gain credibility so that when God needs you to do something for Him, He can use you and doesn't have to find someone else.

Read back over Colossians 3:23-24 and decide specific ways that you can focus on God in your work rather than on the success of your efforts. Do those things.

EXPECTATIONS

READ IT

Knowing Christ has its rewards.

Some people strive to know Christ to make sure they get things, like a get-out-of-hell-free card or their best life now. Some people leave the church and say they left because it didn't work for them. Some people grow bitter when they learn that God has the power to protect but chooses not to. Some people have great expectations for God; however, when He doesn't meet their expectations, they bail. The problem with this entire paragraph is that it is built upon human ideas. None of this comes from scripture.

Paul got it. Paul understood something about knowing Christ. Paul's reaction to whether or not his expectations for God were met didn't change. Paul's expectations changed. He asks for it. He prays for it. He looks for it. And it isn't what you'd expect.

Read Philippians 3:8-14 slowly. Try to take in every sentence like Paul is writing directly to you, hoping you will understand this one thing that will change everything.

After you've read it, ask God, "What am I not getting? Is there something more here for me?" Read it again.

Go back and read verse 10 three more times.

SINK IN IT

Paul didn't have the privilege of walking around with Jesus, learning from Him on earth as a disciple. Paul got to know Christ through the HS, through the testimonies of those that knew Him, through rigorous scripture study and finding Jesus throughout scripture. But still, Paul wants to know Christ. And what is the reward for knowing Him? What does Paul get out of knowing Christ?

The reward is knowing Him.

The reward is Jesus. All of Jesus. There are countless ways that verse ten could have been written. I want to know Christ, the power of His resurrection and participation in walking on water, or healing lepers, or feeding the masses, or teaching with authority, or casting out demons, etc. But that's not what Paul writes. He sums up knowing Christ–all of Christ–in two things, the power of His resurrection and participation in His sufferings. With Jesus, you can't have one without the other. You get both. And Jesus is with you through it.

You want to know Christ? You really want to know Him? You want to count everything as loss and garbage compared to knowing Him? *Everything?* Really? You want to pray to know Him more? You want to sing songs about it? You want to lose your self in Him? You want to press on to grab hold of Him the way He has grabbed ahold of you? Really?

Then you get the whole package. Powerful resurrection and participation in suffering. What did you expect? Seriously. What did you expect? Make a list of the things that you thought you would get out of knowing Christ. If you're going to count everything as loss compared to knowing Him, you need to have a starting point of everything that means nothing compared to the real reward, simply knowing Jesus.

PRAY IT

Tell God how you're feeling. When you think about participating in the suffering and death of Christ, how do you feel? Terrified? Tell Him what is going on in your head and your heart. Tell Him what you believe your limits are. Tell Him how much you want everything to be set right. Tell Him how much you want to know the power of the resurrection. Tell Him how much you are willing to participate in Christ's sufferings if it means that you will really, really, really know Him. Tell Him how much everything is loss compared to knowing Him.

Then, sit in the truth that you are forgetting what is behind, straining for what is ahead, and in the middle of the tension that exists between what has happened and what is to come, you are pressing on.

LIVE IT

Scriptures like Philippians 3 remind us of the big picture in the middle of the mundane and the most massive events. As you go throughout life today and in the week to come, focus on forgetting what is behind, straining for what is ahead, and pressing on. God has brought you through life to this moment, preparing you for what He has prepared for you today. Press on. And in the middle of everything, cling to your one and only legitimate expectation, knowing Christ Jesus, your Lord. He is with you. Walk with Him. Live life with Him. Understand life through the lens of resurrection and suffering. He is your reward now and forever.

EXPERIMENT 25

TESTIMONY

READ IT

Just for reference, read Matthew 2.

Now, read one of the most awesome chapters in the Bible, Revelation 12.

This would be an incredible movie. Michael and his angels fight an enormous red dragon. Seven heads. Ten horns. Seven crowns. Angel armies. Incredible.

But what is more incredible is the whole speech in the middle of the chapter coming from a loud voice in heaven. Write down this speech in your journal.

Notice how Satan is referenced in this speech. He is not called the dragon. He is not called Satan. He is called the accuser.

Notice the who, what and how of the accused.

Who? It is not a single person. It is "they."

What? They overcame. They defeated him. They stood up to the accuser and did not shrink back.

How? With two weapons. First, the blood of the Lamb. The accuser has no power against the blood of the Lamb. Second, their testimony. Their account of the working of the blood of the Lamb in their lives was enough to overcome the accuser.

SINK IN IT

Allow the who, what and how to sink in.

First, they. You were never meant to battle the accuser alone. You need people that are fighting the accuser with you. Other people that are fighting the accuser need you. What is Jesus' word for the group of people that stand together for His purposes to thwart the accuser and move through the world with the message that He is King? Oh yeah. The Church. You need it. They need to know that you are in it with them. You need to know that they are in it with you. The accuser picks off individuals. Don't be an island.

Second, overcame. Accusers aren't much more powerful than the lies that are spoken. He may accuse you of being nasty, unrighteous, and guilty. The Truth says otherwise. You have two very powerful weapons that have been given to you by God.

Third, blood and testimony. There is power in the blood of the Lamb. It covers every accusation. Nasty becomes clean. Unrighteous becomes righteous. Guilty becomes innocent. These give power to your testimony. I was this, but Jesus made me that. I was outcast, but Jesus made me family. I was broken, but Jesus made me fixed. I was dead, but Jesus made me live. I was old, but Jesus made me new.

PRAY IT

Spend some time with Jesus, telling Him that He is the way, the truth and the life. Ask Him to teach you about each of these things. There are things He wants to show you about how those things affect your life. Your testimony is being written. Allow Jesus, the author and perfecter of your life, to rewrite your story, weaving His life into yours, and giving your testimony power. Write out your prayer in your journal and let it wander with truth along the way to life.

LIVE IT

We can't leave the dragon out of this. There is so much more going on than you can imagine in your wildest dreams. Woe to you because you have a target on you as a follower of Christ. Satan has already unleashed an assault on you. It may look just like a Tuesday to you, but it might also look like dragons and angel armies duking it out all around your heart. You won't know until the other side. But every accusation can be met with the blood of the lamb and the word of your testimony.

Write out some simple lines like:

I was _____, but Jesus made me _____.

Tell at least five believers and five non-believers in the next seven days about these statements. Believers need to know because you are with them and they are with you. You are "they." Non-believers need to know because, like David Platt says, every believer this side of heaven owes the gospel to every lost person this side of hell.

ENTITLEMENT

READ IT

Possession is an interesting idea. Kids say the word mine, and they use it like they understand the meaning. Parents, however, know that the kids don't really have anything. Everything is given to them. They are typically only given what they can be trusted with. If a kid throws a cell phone, the parents probably won't trust that kid with a cell phone again. As they get older and with supervision, maybe the parents will trust the phone to the kid. All the while, the kid will insist upon possession with the word mine over and over and over again.

Read Psalm 24:1-2.

Again, possession is an interesting idea. If everything belongs to God, then are we just snotty little kids that insist upon possession with arguments that essentially boil down to mine? Think about how kids understand very little about the big picture. Think about how ungrateful kids are for the amount of unquantifiable care, provision and sacrifice they receive. Think about how kids understand the meaning of entitlement long before they ever learn the word. Are we really all that different?

The big problem here is that it is a very dangerous road. In the passage that follows, money is used to illuminate a heart issue that strays from godliness and contentment, but the idea works for anything that we think we are entitled to.

Read 1 Timothy 6:6-10.

Paul starts with the remedy, the virtue, and the reward. Godliness + Contentment = Real Wealth. The pursuit of other versions of more leave us empty handed at death.

Paul ends with the desire, the warning, and the result. Love + Money = Evil. Notice what he doesn't say. He never says that money is evil. Or even that money is the root of evil. He says that about the love of money. Laying down your life for the sake of money is the root of all kinds of evil.

Satan, desiring evil for your life, doesn't have to get you to serve him, worship him, or bow down to him. All he has to do is get you to love money, and the rest will take care of itself. That is a very dangerous road.

SINK IN IT

Remember, the goal here is godliness with contentment. It starts with recognizing that God owns everything. Picture Him trusting you with everything you've been given. Your stuff. Your talents. Your breath. Your experiences. Your good times. Your hard times. Your love. Your loss. Your life lessons. Your gifts. Your abilities. Your work. Your money. Your hobbies. Your joy. Your regrets. Your season. Your life. None of that is yours. It's God's. He has entrusted that to you.

Sometimes you want more of one thing and less of another. Sometimes you think you deserve more of one thing and less of another. Sometimes you are so focused on the things in front of you (or the lack of things), that entitlement takes the place of gratitude.

When you want the blessings of God more than you want God himself, you are on a dangerous road.

Sink in the fact that every "possession" you have could be taken away in an instant. Sink in your lack of fully appreciating the things that God has entrusted to you. Sink in the truth that everything is His.

PRAY IT

Embrace gratefulness. Start off by listing the things that you are thankful for. You might struggle with what to add to the list around 100 things. This list should easily top 1,000 things, and approach 10,000 over time. Take nothing for granted. Everything is God's, and He has trusted you with millions of His things.

After you have spent some time making a list, ask the hard question: "God, since this is all yours, what do you want me to do with it?"

As God speaks to you, write down some clear things that you know will show Him that He is Lord and that you are pursuing godliness and contentment, not money (or other possessions).

LIVE IT

Take your first steps from what you wrote down in your prayer. Confront discontentment with thankfulness throughout the day. When you begin to feel any discontent, find something to be thankful for and thank God for it. Spend your time zooming out to practice gratefulness rather than entitlement.

Add to your list in some spare time moments today. Instead of your normal time killers like social networks or flinging digital birds, enlarge your list.

STORMS

READ IT

Jesus calms the storm. This is a pretty popular Bible story. It has great significance for our interactions with Jesus in the storms of life. There is definitely more to the story than just the order of events. Read Mark 4:35-41 out loud like you would to entertain a small child.

Write down the conversation part of the story in your journal, quoting the disciples and Jesus.

SINK IN IT

The events are pretty normal at first. It's evening, and they are in a boat. Jesus is sleeping. Makes sense. But there is this storm. And the waves are sinking the boat. The disciples are probably bucketing the water out of the boat after each big wave. Makes sense. They wake up Jesus. More buckets could lead to a better chance of survival. Makes sense. But then they ask Him a question that doesn't help and illuminates their assumptions about Jesus.

They have assumed that this is the end of their lives. For some of these guys, they have lived most of their lives on the water. This must be a bad storm. But when they wake Him, they don't ask for help. They don't ask how He could sleep through such a storm. They assume that His lack of action means that

He doesn't care. They question His heart. They question His motives. And the underlying assumption is that He is powerless to do anything about the storm. He is their last resort, but they don't even ask Him to act. If anything, they expected Him to take care of the storm without being notified that there was a storm.

Then it plays out pretty plainly. They notify Him of the storm while revealing their assumptions about His inabilities. He gets up and deals with the storm. And then He deals with their hearts.

PRAY IT

What are the storms that you're in right now? Have you felt like Jesus is sleeping through them? Have you assumed that He should just fix things without even being notified? Have you assumed that He doesn't care because as far as you can tell, He hasn't acted yet? Are things out of control?

Hear the words of Jesus. "Peace! Quiet! Be Still! Settle Down!"

Tell Jesus about what you are going through. Tell Him how you feel. Be honest. Give Him details.

LIVE IT

In the end, Jesus didn't just deal with the storm, roll His eyes or sigh in frustration and go back to bed, slamming the door of the hull to show his frustration with His disciples. He looks them in the eye and deals with their hearts. Jesus might calm the storm in your life. But more than that, He wants to deal with your heart. He wants to deal with the things that you believe about Him that aren't true.

The disciples questioned whether Jesus cared about them. Jesus. They had no idea that He cared about them more than anyone has cared about anyone in the course of human history. As you go about your day, tell God about stuff, but be aware of your assumptions about the nature of God.

Give God space to call you out and deal with your heart. Give God space to question your motives and your faith. Give God space to teach you about who He is and who you are becoming in Him.

Tonight, before you go to bed, write down the things that God is showing you.

FREE SLAVES

READ IT

Paul is trying to illustrate the difference between life and death as hard as he can in Romans 6.

Read Romans 6:8-12, then stop after 12 and reread that verse.

The weird thing about freedom is that it gives us options. Verse 12 is a hinge pin in this passage. Don't choose to go back. Understand that every time you go back, it's your choice, and you don't have to.

Start reading again and read verses 12-18, then stop after 18 and reread that verse.

Remember, the weird thing about freedom is that it gives us options. Freedom came to you because you put Jesus on the throne of your life. He is in charge and gives freedom. So in this interesting twist, Jesus destroys sin and death, but doesn't destroy the options of sin and death. However, He has enabled the options of life and righteousness. You can't pick and choose though. It's one or the other. That's why he uses slave language.

Read the rest of the chapter.

SINK IN IT

Jesus didn't just come to earth to get us from hell to heaven. Jesus came to get God to us. This has enormous implications for how you live. The problem is that many people that meet Jesus don't let this truth really affect them. So it never affects them.

If you can be sure of anything, be sure that God is all up in your business. When you make the choice to believe that Jesus is Lord of your life, God is relentless, demanding a new slavery to righteousness. And this new slavery exists in and produces freedom.

That is weird. If verse 12 seems more like fantasy than reality to you, then you need to let this affect you: being alive in Jesus is eternal life that started when you surrendered. It doesn't start after your body dies. It has already begun. In order for that to affect your life, you've got to let it affect your heart.

PRAY IT

What's your initial reaction to all of this? Write that down.

Now, ask God why. Is this reaction part of you being alive in Christ or a lingering stench from your old self?

Let God start with your reaction and work backward through your heart to show you the way to freedom.

Let Jesus' death affect your heart so that it will affect your life.

After you've let Him search your heart and show you His, write down these two things:

      1. Your understanding of death to life.

2. How that affects your living.

LIVE IT

Since we now know that we choose our master, God or sin, let's be proactive rather than reactive. Either way, your entire day, week, month, year, and life will be filled with actions. Reactive living settles for what life throws at you. Proactive living discovers freedom in this little thing called abundant life.

Reactive living is hoping to not sin. Ugh. It still reeks of death.

Proactive living is chasing the HS, the guide of your life. Proactive living aligns your heart with His and creates, redeems, liberates and loves the world all around.

Let death to life affect your living today. Tonight, before you go to sleep, get out your journal and finish this sentence:

Alive in Christ isn't just scripture, today it looked like...

SERVE

READ IT

In an often quoted passage in Mark 10, Jesus says that He did not come to be served, but to serve. We understand service within the context of the culture we grow up in. In America, most people that serve get paid to do it. Waiters, butlers, soldiers and policemen all receive money for service. Also, services that benefit society are elevated as noble services. What happens in the upper room isn't like anything we have in our culture.

Read John 13:1-17, focusing on Jesus' tone.

Jesus is modeling servant leadership. Jesus serves them by washing their feet. He isn't looking for what He can get out of it. He isn't looking for a merit badge or a purple heart. In verse 12, He links what He has just done with what He will do by asking a question. He then goes on to teach them about service. Notice how absurd verse 14 sounds. Jesus just washed their feet. At this point, their feet are clean. No need for foot washing. But He says that they should wash one another's feet.

Foot washing was a very specific role in society. Not one of the disciples was following Jesus or climbing the proverbial ladder to end up as a foot washer. This was a position that someone settled for or was forced to endure. Jesus says to choose it.

SINK IN IT

Service has all sorts of conditions wrapped around it in our culture, even amongst Christians. When given the opportunity to serve, you ask questions like "Do I have that time free? Would I like to do that? Who else is going to be there? Is it a fundraiser? Do I really support the mission and vision of that organization? Is this part of my gifting? How long is it going to take? Are there going to be refreshments?"

Jesus doesn't ask these questions. He is motivated by love of people and service is a byproduct. And He doesn't just love those who love Him. He grabs His towel and gets on His knees, and washes the feet of the most disloyal, dishonest, dirty man that will be the death of Him—Judas.

Sink in that for a second. Question every justification you've ever had for not serving. Understand the pride shift that has to happen to be a follower of Jesus.

PRAY IT

In David Crowder Band's song *All I Can Say*, David sings a verse that personalizes this story. Imagine that after all the things you've done wrong and all the things you've yet to do wrong, that Jesus still serves you.

> *I didn't notice You were standing here // I didn't know that that was You holding me // I didn't notice You were cry'n too // I didn't know that that was You washing my feet*

He washes your dirt.

Pray through what is going on in your head and your heart right now. Does this make you feel good, bad or indifferent? Why?

LIVE IT

Jesus gives us an incredible example here, serving without regard to whether or not they deserve to be served. Today, ask "How can I help others?" Do it. Don't figure out if they should be helped out or not. Just do it. In fact, if you find yourself judging whether or not someone deserves your service, go above and beyond to help them, praying for them and that God will change your heart. Identify moments where you aren't seeing people the way that Jesus does. Do something that He would do to make yourself less by serving them.

Don't let this just be a one day thing. As the HS leads you, work this into the natural rhythm of your life.

HEAVEN

READ IT

What is heaven? An afterlife? An eternal life? Harps and clouds and togas and streets of gold?

Heaven is a Kingdom. Heaven has a King. And heaven is here.

Read Luke 17:20-21.

Jesus is Lord. He is the King. And the Kingdom is here right now, within you. If He is your King. Following Christ is learning how to live in the Kingdom. It's new, so it's not old. It's pain free, so it's full of love. It is here now and it's on it's way. Learn the new ways of living as a part of the Kingdom.

Paying special attention to the lists, read Colossians 3:1-17 three times.

For all the believers to be together in heaven, we have to live new. We can't bring all the stuff from our old lives in with us. What Jesus makes clear, and Paul emphasizes in his letter to the Colossians, is that nothing from the old life gets to come with us into the Kingdom, and the Kingdom is now. Eternal life doesn't start when your physical body dies. It starts when you are spiritually born again. The old is gone, the new has come. Act like it.

SINK IN IT

You are not who you were. One of the frustrations is that even though you have been given a new life, you are still a part of creation which is under the curse from the fall. God has sent the HS to give you new life and change your heart and mind. You are no longer a slave to sin because you are a child of God, a citizen in the Kingdom of Heaven.

Paul gives very specific instructions about your old life. He uses words like, rid yourself of, put to death, killing off, take off, stripped off and gone for good. Another way to say it is murder your old life. You can't do this by yourself. You weren't meant to. And if you try to on your own, you are belittling the cross of Christ and the blood of Jesus.

Your old life, your sinful nature, who you were is not destroyed by your will power, your strength, or your commitment to controlling your self. It is destroyed by the blood of Jesus. That's where the real power is. You couldn't fix yourself. He climbed on your cross to set you free.

PRAY IT

Talk to God about the old life lists. Pray through the examples that Paul wrote about your old life. Get out of the examples and into the specifics. Tell God about how you are each of those things. Remember the specific details about the events in your life that Paul generalized in those lists.

Chances are that some of the things on those lists still linger around. Chances are that you haven't murdered those things. Chances are that you have tried to control your old self instead of letting Christ take those on the cross with Him and killing them there. Give those things up to Jesus. Tell Him He can

110

have the list of things from your old life. Walk through the list slowly, giving Him each thing on it.

Then, ask for the HS to teach you each thing on the new life lists. Don't assume that you know these things. And understand that when you ask to learn things like patience, He will put you in situations that require patience. When you ask to learn humility, you will have the chance to humble yourself. He will teach you and remind you of everything that Jesus taught.

LIVE IT

Having the HS is heaven. The HS is your new heartbeat. Sometimes it is calm. Sometimes it is racing. Sometimes you forget it's even there. Hold onto this: the HS is pumping new life through you.

Live new. Listen as one being taught. When you sense your old life reaching for your heart, remind it that it was crucified with Christ. It is powerless, old, dead, and done.

Give the HS your ears today as He guides you throughout your day, convincing you that you are new, and leading you in the way everlasting.

REMAIN

READ IT

Never quit.   This last month has marked you.   You will remember this month for the rest of your life.   The work God has done in your heart is good, strong, and sure.   But He isn't done.

Read John 15:3-4.

These are simple words from Jesus.   They are so important. For some reason, we need these words.   Jesus has cleaned us through the washing of His Word in our lives.   For some reason we need the encouragement, urging and reminder that we must remain in Him in order for Him to remain in us.   We cannot drift.   We cannot wander.   We must remain.

You're not done.   You have more to do.   Remaining requires effort.

SINK IN IT

In For the Love of God: Volume 2 by D. A. Carson, he talks about this effort and the effects of not remaining in Him.

> *"People do not drift toward holiness. Apart from grace-driven effort, people do not gravitate toward godliness, prayer, obedience to Scripture, faith, and delight in the Lord. We drift toward*

compromise and call it tolerance; we drift toward
disobedience and call it freedom; we drift toward
superstition and call it faith. We cherish the
indiscipline of lost self-control and call it
relaxation; we slouch toward prayerlessness and
delude ourselves into thinking we have escaped
legalism; we slide toward godlessness and
convince ourselves we have been liberated."

This is precisely the future that you don't want. He says "apart from grace driven effort" and writes the end of the choose-your-own-adventure story that you don't want to choose.

Spending time with God every day is a choice you make. Filling that time with something else may not feel like a choice, but it is. And it is the opposite of remaining.

Getting up every day and getting on your face and thanking God for the mercy He has shown you and begging that He use your life to bring glory to His Kingdom and His great Name doesn't just happen.

But don't miss what Jesus (and Carson) are saying. Jesus cleaned you; now, grace drives the effort. If it ever reverses, effort driven grace, it isn't Jesus. That's not how He works. Once you've received grace, it changes the way you live. It drives you to remain. You don't try really hard to remain so that you will get grace.

PRAY IT

Thank God for saving you. Thank Him for His infinite mercy. Ask Him to break you open so that people will know the Love that has changed you. Get on your face and beg for Him to be glorified in and through your life. Ask Him to wring glory out of your life. However hard the wringing, commit to perseverance. Let Him have you, and in turn you'll find that you continue to have Him.

LIVE IT

Now is the beginning of the rest of your life. It's not you against the world, and you have to figure out how to make it work. It's you, together with God, with Jesus, with the HS, with the church against the world. Never quit.

Tell some people. Do the things you wrote down throughout this month. Never quit. If you need to, go back and read it again. Share it. Tell your story. Give God glory. Billions of people don't know Christ. You do. It can't end with you. Remain in Him. This dark world needs Him. Shine. Live bright. Live love. Live new.

ABOUT THE AUTHOR

My name is Kurt Libby. I live in Oroville, CA with my beautiful wife Rhonda and our two kids, Bella and Jace. I pastor the students at Oroville Nazarene Church and direct a youth center non-profit called The Axiom.

Much of this book is from my journals, from my quiet times, and the things that God has taught me about living new over the last 14 years. Putting the finishing details on this book and adding this brief piece about me is surreal. 5 years ago I was teaching Algebra and Physics at a local high school. Jesus worked hard, climbing every step of my life to dethrone my ego and has called me to preach the good news. I have no confidence in my ability, but in His mercy, He has given me the competence in the HS. I hope that God speaks to you out of His Word, that you heard His voice when you read through these pages, and that you have fallen more in love with Him.

Like it says in the SUCCESS experiment, I won't measure this book by how well it sells or how many tweets it generates, but I have found my fulfillment in obeying His voice. He is always at work, even right now, and I pray that these words will spur you on to acts of love and good deeds.

I hope that someday we can sit down and you can share with me how God has enabled you to live new. If we've never met, I hope to hear your story, on this side or the next. And if we are friends, I cannot thank you enough for the ways that you have encouraged and challenged me to pursue God wholeheartedly.

Please connect with me and share your story. And share your daily victories on twitter with the hashtag #livenew. I look forward to hearing all about it.

--Kurt Libby

twitter.com/livenewbook

facebook.com/livenewbook

misterlib.com

www.ingramcontent.com/pod-product-compliance
Lightning Source LLC
Chambersburg PA
CBHW021131020426
42331CB00005B/722